D1349461

THE RALLYING IMPREZAS

THE RALLYING IMPREZAS

DAVID WILLIAMS FOREWORD BY DAVID RICHARDS

Haynes Publishing

© David Williams 2004

First published in November 2004

All rights reserved. No part of this publication may be reproduced
or stored in a retrieval system or transmitted, in any form or by
any means, electronic, mechanical, photocopying, recording or
otherwise, without prior permission in writing from
the publisher.

David Williams has asserted his right to
be identified as the author of this work

Photography by McKlein

A catalogue record for this book is
available from the British Library

ISBN 1 84425 093 8

Library of Congress catalog card no. 2004106168

Published by Haynes Publishing, Sparkford,
Yeovil, Somerset, BA22 7JJ, UK
Tel: 01963 442030 Fax: 01963 440001
Int. tel: +44 1963 442030 Fax: +44 1963 440001
E-mail: sales@haynes.co.uk
Website: www.haynes.co.uk

Haynes North America, Inc.
861 Lawrence Drive, Newbury Park,
California 91320, USA

Designed & typeset by G&M Designs Limited,
Raunds, Northamptonshire, England
Printed and bound in England by
J. H. Haynes & Co. Ltd, Sparkford

Contents

Foreword
by David Richards
Chairman, Prodrive

In 1989, when the partnership between Subaru in Japan and Prodrive in England first started, the Impreza was still on the drawing board and we had no idea what an impact it would ultimately have on the World Rally Championship and the fortunes of Subaru itself.

We were, after all, two relatively small companies on opposite sides of the world joined by a common goal and taking on the might of some of the biggest factory teams that the World Rally Championship has ever seen.

The success of this project is a testament to the extraordinary co-operation that was established between these two groups of people who shared a dream that many thought impossible.

The Subaru Impreza has become, without doubt, an icon of the World Rally Championship, a tribute to the ingenuity and skills of a very dedicated group of engineers separated by both culture and geography yet sharing one passion. It is to this group of talented engineers and technicians that this book should truly be dedicated.

Acknowledgements

No book of this kind is a solo effort and I am indebted to a large cast, many of whom have contributed repeatedly and generously. I'm afraid that the following list, while long, may not be complete. If I have missed anyone, I apologise. In the meantime, I'm glad to single out Sarah Ansley, Simon Baker, Jules Bigg, Richard Burns, David Campion, Kenneth Eriksson, Pierre-Yves Genon, Anne Gigney, John Hardaker, Graham Holmes, Paul Howarth, Juha Kankkunen, Reinhard Klein, David Lapworth, Christian Loriaux, Bob McCaffrey, Alan McGuinness, Colin McMaster, Colin McRae, John McLean, Graham Moore, Flora Myer, Ken Rees, Robert Reid, David Richards, Nigel Riddle, Carlos Sainz, Martin Sharp, Petter Solberg, John Spiller, Katie Tweedle, Tony Welam, Steve Webb and Steve Wilson.

Introduction

The flags catch the eye first. Petter Solberg's swashbuckling successes on the Rally of Great Britain have led to the creation of a hybrid, part Norway's blue cross on its red background and part the red dragon of Wales, in recognition of his co-driver Phil Mills. But look more closely at the fans and you'll notice many of them are also wearing blue and yellow clothing, the colours of the works Subarus.

In fact, the livery evolved not in Japan, but in Britain, as they were the chosen colours of 555 when British American Tobacco sponsored the team. They became so closely identified with the Impreza rally cars that when the sponsorship deal ended, the colour scheme endured. Indeed, by some estimates, Subaru's identity is more widely recognised than any Formula 1 team's colours other than Ferrari's. It's a remarkable achievement for a relatively small Japanese car maker and a tribute to Subaru's astonishing rise in arguably the most demanding form of motorsport.

When it embarked on a full-blooded international rally programme at the very end of the 1980s, Subaru was a little-known producer of quirky cars – the perfect material for an obscure motoring quiz – contemplating its own demise. Profits were being squeezed and it couldn't make the economies of scale of its giant rivals. Motorsport, principally rallying, seemed the best means of branding itself on the public consciousness worldwide and demonstrating the strengths of Subaru engineering, in particular four-wheel drive.

In the years since, it has won six world rally titles and countless lesser championships across the globe, from Ireland to Norway, Poland to Italy, the USA to Australia. It has transformed itself into a brand with a cult following, whose road and rally cars thrive on the same attributes. Its success has been a triumph of marketing and engineering in tandem, in which competition has genuinely highlighted the merits of the production car rather than bestowing a veneer of glamour on a mundane industrial appliance.

This success has been gained overwhelmingly with one car: the Impreza. Ask an engineer to sketch his ideal rally car and the chances are that the result will owe a good deal to the Subaru. Since its launch in 1993, the Impreza has become the epitome of rally car design. A compact saloon equipped with four-wheel drive from the outset, it is a car built around its engine. The flat-four is highly tuneable, but it is also small and light, sited low down and longitudinally in the car's nose. Whereas most of its rivals tend to be nose-heavy compromises originally created with front-wheel drive and family motoring in mind, its engine and transaxle give an Impreza ideally balanced weight distribution. It is equally at home on the car-breaking back roads of Greece and Kenya, or the tortuous, mountainous asphalt of Corsica.

Some of the world's greatest rally cars gained a reputation for being difficult to handle; indeed, it became part of their mystique. That has never applied to the Impreza. As an engineer's car, it is naturally also a driver's car, and perhaps its outstanding merit is that it has been supremely adaptable, suiting drivers as

By 1995, the Impreza had become the car to beat in any conditions and in Catalonia, Colin McRae waged a dramatic duel with his teammate, the ultimate victor Carlos Sainz.

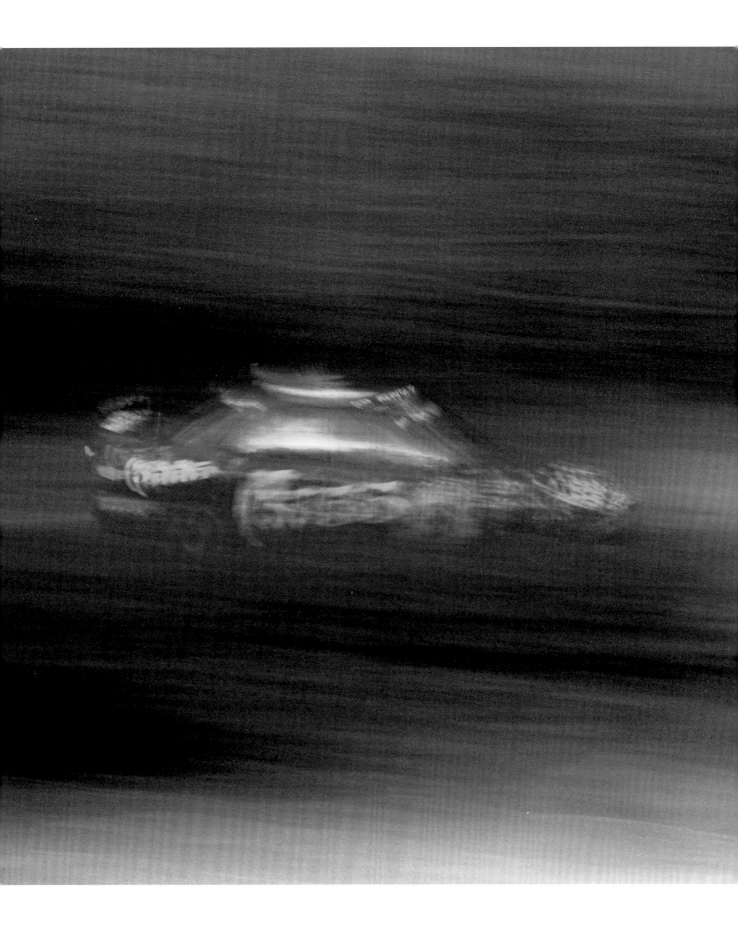

different as Colin McRae, Carlos Sainz and Petter Solberg. Partly for that reason, it has won almost every major rally it has contested. Only one other car has a comparable record, the Lancia Delta. Nothing could be more appropriate, for Subaru makes the kind of ingenious, distinctive sports saloons that Lancia built in its heyday.

Naturally, the Impreza has evolved greatly, reflecting the demands of competition and the marketplace. A 21st-century Impreza World Rally Car doesn't share many parts with its 1993 ancestor, yet the fundamental characteristics remain the same. The engine, much refined, is essentially the original design, while both the suspension and the transmission layout are recognisably from the same blueprint. The design has stood the test of time.

Nonetheless, the Impreza's success has been achieved against the odds. There have been plenty of rally cars that have succeeded in spite of their limitations. At its highest level, the sport is a battleground for big manufacturers, in which spending power

In Colin McRae, Subaru found a driver to take it to new heights. In return, he was provided with cars that could take almost unlimited punishment.

and good organisation often tell. Development matters as much as design and development can be bought, along with the best drivers.

Subaru has invariably been the smallest competitor ever since it committed itself wholeheartedly to rallying at the very end of the 1980s. It has had to rely on inspiration, commitment and teamwork. It has consistently made the most of limited resources, creating an Anglo-Japanese partnership with Prodrive that has endured and strengthened.

Success has never been automatic. Competition has been fiercer in the past ten years than at any time in the sport's history. Occasionally, Subaru has gone close to a year without a win, it has sued its lead driver, been riven by bitter rows between teammates and headed for home after rallies in which disaster arrived swiftly and mercilessly. But it has never been on the defensive for long. It is not so much involved as immersed in rallying and, as a result, the best drivers have regularly wanted to drive Imprezas. Like Ferrari, it has become an intrinsic part of its chosen sport.

Subaru supreme: Petter Solberg led the 2004 Rally Japan from start to finish.

1 Starting with something big

To begin the story of the Impreza rally cars without mentioning the Legacy would be like starting a book in mid-sentence. The Impreza was closely related to its forerunner and shared many of its attributes, yet despite its merits, the Legacy was a curate's egg of a rally car. Plenty of its rivals also had four or five doors – the all-conquering Delta Integrale, for instance – but the Subaru was on the large side of medium and competition soon exposed a number of failings.

When it was launched in 1990, the Legacy was a gigantic leap for Subaru, the equivalent of swapping a biplane for a jet fighter. One of Japan's smaller car makers, Subaru was an offshoot of Fuji Heavy Industries, a conglomerate derived from the Nakajima Aircraft Company; it had taken its present name in 1945. Subaru didn't start making cars until 1958 and didn't export them to Britain until 1976 or to the United States until 1977. Although it had been involved in rallying for seven years, it had no great reputation for making cars with any sports potential.

By the time its cars were sold abroad, Subaru had settled on the layout for which it is best known today. They had longitudinally mounted, flat-four engines and many of them were four-wheel drive. The blueprint had been adopted in 1972 with the Subaru 1400 4WD, a pushrod-engined machine with part-time four-wheel drive, sometimes known as the Leone 4WD Estate. The company ventured into international rallying in 1983, with the ebullient New Zealander 'Possum' Bourne, three years before it unveiled its first full-time, four-wheel-drive road car; another Leone.

Although it was an auspicious start, it would be fair to say that it didn't hog the headlines: Bourne romped to victory in the Group A class on his home round of the World Championship, but Group A was in only its second season as an international category and so poorly supported that it was merged with the older but quicker Group 2 class. Bourne's RX Coupé had four-wheel drive, just like the dominant Quattros, but it was hamstrung by a chronic lack of power and, while Group A permitted extensive modifications, Bourne reckoned that the 'tuned' engine was no better than standard. He made his local rivals sit up and take notice with a stunning victory in the snow on the Southland Rally later in the season, when he passed three cars on one stage, but it was an isolated success that owed a good deal to the conditions. He became a much more formidable opponent locally when the RX gained a pair of downdraught Weber carburettors, and Subaru followed that with turbocharged versions of the RX in a variety of body styles.

The extra power did more justice to the chassis, and in favourable circumstances the RX was a regular class winner, taking Group A on the Safari in 1985 and 1986 through Carlo Vitulli and Mike Kirkland respectively. However, with 180bhp at most, it was never going to trouble either the vastly more potent Group B cars that ruled the roost – and had more than 500bhp in some cases – nor for that matter the best Group A cars when Group B was banned and the saloon category gained premier status by default in 1987.

Subaru was one of the first manufacturers to commit itself to four-wheel-drive in international rallying, but rarely had much to show for its efforts with cars such as the RX Turbo. Mike Kirkland's convincing Group A win on the 1986 Safari was an exception rather than the rule.

As its sleeker outline promised, the Legacy was markedly more sophisticated. Whereas its predecessors had had two valves per cylinder and one camshaft per bank of cylinders, the Legacy had 16 valves and four cams. It had MacPherson strut suspension with generous travel all round. The version used for rallying, the RS, had a turbocharger from the start. At a glance, it was a match for anything that Lancia, Toyota or Ford could produce.

The decision to make an all-out World Rally Championship assault was also a landmark for the company and owed a great deal to Ryuichiro Kuze. In the late 1980s, Subaru also dabbled in Formula 1, sponsoring rather than producing an engine. The engine's chief attraction – indeed, pretty much its only attraction – was that it was also horizontally opposed, albeit with 12 cylinders rather than four.

A shrewd, genial man with a toothy grin, Kuze was responsible for preparing a Legacy for a series of long-distance circuit records.

Both that and the F1 episode convinced him that Subaru would be better off in rallying and he played a large part in persuading the company to plan a whole-hearted World Rally Championship campaign, on the basis that it was a field in which four-wheel drive took centre stage. He also highlighted the need for Subaru's own performance label, much like RS at Ford or M Sport for BMW. He therefore became President when Subaru Tecnica International, usually known as STi, was established in April 1988. Rallying would go hand in hand with an increased emphasis on four-wheel drive and high performance.

On both counts, Kuze decided that Subaru needed a European partner. At the highest level, rallying is primarily a European sport and no Japanese manufacturer had enjoyed consistent, worldwide success without a European team. Kuze had been impressed with Prodrive when he visited the 1000 Lakes Rally in Finland and approached the British firm in 1989.

The Legacy always looked the part, but while Markku Alén instantly demonstrated its promise on its first appearance, the Acropolis soon exposed a range of weaknesses.

The Legacy programme represented just as big an opportunity to Prodrive as it did to Subaru. In essence, the British firm applied Formula 1 principles to rallying. Traditionally, a works team was just that: it was a branch of the parent company, based in a small factory of its own or a corner of a much bigger plant. Its staff were as much a part of Ford, Lancia or Skoda as their colleagues on the production line. Prodrive was robustly independent and had more in common with Williams or McLaren. When it was set up as David Richards Autosport in 1984, it had an agreement with Porsche to run cars in the European, Middle East and Irish Tarmac Rally Championships, but it relied equally heavily on Rothmans, which supported all its programmes. Its founder, David Richards, had co-driven Ari Vatanen to the World Championship in 1981 and co-ordinated rally programmes for Fiat in Britain as well as Rothmans in the Middle East, but he was an entrepreneur as much as an enthusiast, with a grounding in

accountancy and a taste for helicopters. Far more than many of his rivals, he understood the importance of image and presentation.

Prodrive has grown into a much larger and more diverse organisation with a substantial engineering division that works for a range of manufacturers, as well as an offshoot in Australia; a large minority shareholding was sold off to the venture capitalists, Apax Partners, in 1997. Richards diversified too, into Formula 1 with BAR and into sports marketing as the holder of the World Rally Championship television rights. But Prodrive remains a company in his image, driven by his restless, ceaseless energy.

These possibilities were not uppermost in the minds of his seven original mechanics. When they joined in January 1984, there was no workshop of any kind. After premises had been found at Silverstone, their first task was to equip an empty building and the first workbench was rescued from the bonfire after it had been thrown out by Alan Docking Racing. On stage, it soon emerged

There's a fine line between exploiting snowbanks and overdoing it. Markku Alén flirted with danger on his way to a morale-boosting second place on the 1991 Swedish.

Nordic drivers customarily made mincemeat of visitors on the Swedish. They were stunned – and full of admiration – when Colin McRae finished second on the 1992 rally.

that the Weissach-designed 911 needed extensive bracing to discourage the front third from parting company with the rest of the car.

The new outfit found its feet very quickly. Richards had hired one of the fastest and most charismatic drivers in the world, the Finn Henri Toivonen, and the team quickly began to win rallies and championships, the latter chiefly in the Middle East and Ireland. When it became apparent that Prodrive's enthusiasm for developing the 959 was not shared at Porsche, it switched to Metro 6R4s in 1986 and came close to winning the British Open Championship with Jim McRae. The Group B ban left Richards with a clutch of expensive, unsold 6R4s and took his fledgling firm within a whisker of bankruptcy. He responded by adroitly negotiating a deal with BMW that netted the team its first World Championship rally win, a magnificent success on the 1987 Tour of Corsica with Bernard Béguin, and took it into racing as well. The BMW deal was accompanied by the name change to Prodrive, which had originally been a driver management company with Toivonen and the Swede, Per Eklund, on its books.

BMW was as half-hearted about rallying as Porsche and while the M3 was a prolific winner on Tarmac, two-wheel drive ensured that it was never the basis of a World Championship contender. However, the late 1980s were in no sense wasted years for Prodrive. It moved into larger premises in Banbury in 1987 and established the nucleus of a highly effective team, directed by Richards, managed by experienced rallymen such as David Campion, Charles Reynolds and John Spiller, with engineering under the control of another of its earliest employees, David Lapworth. It established a reputation for slickly turned-out professionalism and a ferocious workrate. Contesting three or four rallies and races per weekend was far from unusual. More than most, this was a team that lived out of a suitcase.

It was clearly ready for something bigger and better than the M3. When Kuze commenced negotiations, he was welcomed with open arms.

In fact, the Legacy's first rally was as much a continuation of the old era as the start of the new. The 1990 Safari cars were built and run from Japan under the direction of Noriyuki Koseki, another Subaru stalwart,

whose eyepatch gave him a vaguely piratical air. The production origins of car and team were unmistakable. On the most punishing round of the World Championship, the mechanics had to be encouraged to check for loose nuts and bolts, rather than simply reattaching wheels at service points.

In Banbury, in September 1989, a very different car had begun to take shape. Group A rules stipulated that a minimum of 5,000 cars were produced annually and required some resemblance to the standard machine – idiosyncratically, in some respects, demanding standard water pumps and valve sizes, for instance – yet allowing more or less unlimited freedom of everything from camshafts to gearboxes. Lapworth, ably assisted by Bob Farley and John Piper, made the most of these opportunities.

The engine remained STi's responsibility. Everything else was down to Prodrive: as the rules dictated, the suspension layout remained broadly standard, but every component was redesigned from scratch. Bilstein supplied dampers, AP bigger brakes and, in concert with Hewland, Prodrive devised a six-speed gearbox. For speed and strength, it was non-synchromesh, in contrast

to the production-derived five-speeder used on the Safari. It owed something to the five-speed design used in the Group B Metro 6R4, as both Farley and Piper had had a hand in creating the MG. Elements of it survived into the 2004 World Rally Car, yet time was so tight that parts of the original were being made while others were still being designed.

Minimal weight was one of the priorities, ease of servicing another. The intention was that just two bolt sizes would be used throughout the car, and that any part other than the engine could be replaced in 15 minutes. It was designed to force the pace technically as well. At the time, most teams relied on a viscous coupling centre differential. The silicon-based fluid ensured that it locked and unlocked in a predictable and reasonably benign manner, but it had limited scope for adjustment. The Legacy transmission appeared with three clutch-type differentials, but before it had even contested a rally, there were hints that active control of the differentials, the next major leap in performance, would be introduced within months.

Active systems had already been used in Formula 1, in which bigger budgets and a far

In the early 1990s, most works teams regarded a top Finn as indispensable. When Alén left, Ari Vatanen stepped into the breach for Subaru.

smaller number of corners facilitated the use of advanced technology. In 1990, manipulating differential behaviour seemed an invitation to unreliability as much as increased performance in rallying.

But there were a few other hurdles to clear before stepping up transmission development: showing the car to senior management in Japan, then to the press in Britain and finally, confronting the opposition on the Acropolis Rally.

More than a decade on, Nigel Riddle, then the chief mechanic, could just about recall the Japanese trip without a shudder.

'We went out to this place, shrouded in bloody secrecy, in the middle of nowhere. We had a day or so to get the car running and prepared. We polished it and sort of titivated it about: "We'll just run it down the road to make sure it steers straight," and the bonnet came up and broke the windscreen. Just the thing you dread happening!

'They got us another screen, but they couldn't do much for the bonnet, so we had to straighten that ourselves. We got another screen, plugged that in and away we went, did our demos the following day, which was all and sundry, including giving the President a ride up and down in it,' he said.

Proceedings were interrupted briefly after a front wishbone sheared when the car was revealed to the press in a forest opposite Silverstone, in fact, but the sense of optimism was unshakeable. This was the car that Prodrive had longed for and as if to prove that there would be no half-measures, Markku Alén had been recruited to drive it. By 1990, team managers were no longer fighting tooth and nail to get the gangling Finn's name on a contract, but he remained one of the sport's biggest attractions – no one had won more World Championship rallies at the time – and a turn of speed that would have done justice to an electric hare had not deserted him. While conceding that it was a touch short of power, Alén enthused about the handling. It reminded him of a Volvo 142, he said – which was no backhanded compliment – and he expected it to be competitive by the 1000 Lakes in August.

Adapting to new circumstances wasn't an entirely straightforward process for team or driver. After 16 years with Fiat and Lancia, Alén was liable to pull in at Lancia service points before being sent politely on his way, and on the Acropolis, at the beginning of June 1990, there was abundant scope to give vent to a famously Latin temperament.

'I expect if we were honest with ourselves, we felt a bit out of our depth at the time, because the opposition was Lancia and Toyota,' Riddle commented. 'We were very ambitious to be taking those boys on! The first few events were just mind-blowingly difficult really. You just couldn't believe how you could have one problem after another after another. All those involved still talk about the first Acropolis, because it was like a bloody battlefield really. We led on the super special, thinking, "This is an easy business!"

'Three days of hell, absolute hell. I've probably never worked so hard in my life. We were whizzing about in helicopters and we didn't know what was going to break next. But jolly good fun.'

It had been an ambitious choice of baptism. The Acropolis was rightly notorious as the most destructive rally in Europe. That year's covered 1,263 miles, with 48 stages totalling 368 miles, a substantial proportion of them on little used and therefore pitilessly rough roads near Athens. The Legacy first ran into trouble on the second stage, when the front suspension and a driveshaft worked loose. The suspension had become loose again by SS4 and in the end the mechanics resorted to welding the castor-adjustment spacers into the wishbones; never mind the adjustment, the priority was making sure the wheels didn't fall off. The turbo boost fluctuated, the gearbox went sick, the dampers went soft, but Alén plugged on until the engine gave up the ghost nine stages from the end.

The car could scarcely be described as competitive. It was intermittently quick, Alén leading the RAC Rally briefly, but it was too short of power to finish higher than fourth on the 1000 Lakes, when he sampled three different gearbox specifications – including a viscous coupling – and it was dogged by transmission, suspension and engine problems. It finished only one World Championship round in its first season and Subaru scored more points from less potent five-speed cars.

Yet there was no thought that new technology could wait while the defects were rooted out. By the Sanremo Rally that October, low-pressure hydraulic and electronic control had been introduced to the centre differential, the first step towards a fully active transmission. The data logger already mapped 36 parameters, although it had a tiny memory by modern standards of 32KB. Four of those elements, throttle angle, turbo boost, braking and ground speed, were fed into the ECU that controlled the transmission; it was unable to handle more than one element at a time.

It was an open-loop or passive control system, which meant that it could react to the parameters measured by the ECU, but, unlike an active system, it could not be programmed to respond to those parameters by performing in a predetermined manner.

François Chatriot, a Prodrive stalwart and a former French Champion in its BMWs, was offered a second car and he provided a little more testing insight than Alén, whose commitment wasn't matched by his powers of analysis.

The chassis was evidently very good indeed. The engine was another matter. Power outputs have been difficult to establish accurately since the start of the Group A era, because the FIA accompanied the Group B ban with a power limit of 300bhp. It is entirely notional, never measured and capriciously applied. Prudent manufacturers have therefore claimed no more than 300bhp regardless of engine development, turbocharger dimensions or turbocharger

Few Legacys absorbed as much punishment as Colin McRae's 1992 1000 Lakes car. It withstood three rolls (one before the event) on its way to a memorable eighth place.

restrictor size. But when the Legacy appeared, it is safe to say that it barely exceeded the 'limit' in the most favourable circumstances and that it was sometimes 100bhp short of its main rivals. As the engine management system was programmed to retard the ignition, cut boost and thereby power at the first hint of springlike temperatures, Alén's frustration periodically boiled over. The engine was none too reliable either. Connecting rod bolts in particular were prone to failure.

Alén got the team's second season off to a flying start with a fine second place on the Swedish, in sub-zero conditions that didn't place too much strain on the flat-four, but this success wasn't repeated elsewhere and, although he led the 1000 Lakes fleetingly, he had become so fed up with the engine that he signed for Toyota a week after his home rally, albeit for a solitary season.

There were plenty of long nights in the workshop, and it might have become a dispiriting as well as a laborious business if Richards hadn't devised a means of planning for the future and raising morale. The answer could be summed up in two words, indelibly associated with the Impreza: Colin McRae.

A better-established team might have decided against signing the 23-year-old Scot in 1991, even purely for the British Open Championship. There was no denying that he was quick, but he was erratic too and British rally drivers were as poorly regarded internationally as British tennis players. The cynical view was that Jim McRae's oldest son was cannon fodder like all the rest, but high maintenance with it.

Richards has never pretended that he recognised at once that McRae had the capability to win a record number of World Championship rallies, but he identified something out of the ordinary.

'There were lots of reasons why it was the right thing for us to do, because the team was very young and yet we were going off and doing World Championship rallies,' Richards said. 'I needed to have a secondary series, a secondary championship going as development and testing of the car, so the

British series provided that. And also it was going to be very difficult for us to get results in the World Championship at the time with the car, but boosting morale by winning British events on our home soil would keep everyone afloat and keep everything going, so that was my internal objective.

'I suppose I saw in Colin many of the attributes I saw in Ari. There is an extraordinary, single-minded approach to everything he does, an extraordinary self-conviction that all top sportsmen possess, that you have to have if you're going to the very top.'

British Championship rallies were shorter and, like the opposition, less taxing. McRae won first time out, on the 1991 Cartel Rally in the Yorkshire forests, and galloped to the British title two years running. By late 1992, he was sometimes capable of flaying the opposition by a minute per stage. He had also become part of the World Championship team. He stunned the rally world by finishing second on the 1992 Swedish – an event that remained the exclusive preserve of Finns and Swedes for another decade – and proved quite capable of keeping Alén and Vatanen on their toes.

The Swedish wasn't simply a breakthrough for McRae. Following a successful test with Vatanen in Finland, it was also the first time that Prodrive used a truly active centre differential in competition – a development that generated rather fewer headlines, even though it had even more long-term significance. Hydraulics and electronics had progressed jointly to the stage at which they could monitor and adjust a differential's behaviour constantly, in a closed loop.

The more sophisticated transmission had been planned from the outset, but there had been all kinds of other problems to tackle first. The Finnish test was merely the culmination of an exhaustive development programme, much of it a hard slog at MIRA, the British industry's development track near Nuneaton. It was a bold step, for hydraulic differentials had often been temperamental in other rally cars and Lancia, then the team to beat, never risked using them in competition.

As the British series was a 'semi-works' programme, Prodrive had more room for manoeuvre and McRae therefore began using a British- rather than a Japanese-tuned version of the EJ20 flat-four. Remapping the electronics had instantly released another 40bhp on the test bed. It led to another engine failure too, but confirmed what Prodrive had suspected, that the unit's potential was not being exploited to the full.

When Alén retired from the 1992 1000 Lakes with another dead engine, Richards decided that enough was enough. It was agreed that Prodrive would build the engines for the RAC, and Graham Moore, Lapworth's deputy, was told that he had three months to prove that he could do better than STi. He had started work on the engine, assisted by Bill King and Nigel Strange, just five months previously. His background, in a company that hadn't previously employed engine builders, made him the natural choice. He had worked on engines with Taurus Engineering in Bournemouth, but had also been involved with the Ministry of Defence, working for Westland and Wellington Wiring, on both helicopters and an electronically controlled system for tracking

incoming missiles; he stresses that he confined himself to defensive rather than offensive equipment.

Prodrive had no dynamometer at the time – an essential tool for development – and therefore resorted initially either to one at Cowley or another at Andy Rouse's premises in Southam. There wasn't time to make many special parts and, mercifully, no real need either. New suppliers were found for con rod bolts and pistons, and Moore decided that Wills rings would be preferable to head gaskets. There were some modifications to internal water flow too.

'We did away with the head gasket. That helped us in a few other areas as well and that seemed to make the engine fairly bomb-proof after that. A couple of the drivers did test it, driving it without any water in it for a few ks. It wasn't completely indestructible. You could get away with quite a few – so long as it had oil in it. If you'd lost the oil, forget it, but if the oil was still in and the cooler was still working, 200 degrees oil temperature, I've seen them recover, which is pretty amazing,' Moore said.

The transformation of the EJ20's reputation had begun, but Moore's

It had been on the cards for months, but the 1993 New Zealand victory, the first at World Championship level for Subaru and for Colin McRae, was a momentous, nerve-shredding feat nevertheless.

immediate priority was merely to get three engines assembled. STi supplied new turbos, but the RAC engines were built in large measure from parts left over from previous blow-ups.

McRae led for much of the way, only to fall foul of a puncture and a transmission problem in his bogey forest, Grizedale, leaving Vatanen to finish second to Carlos Sainz's Celica. The point was taken. Prodrive would henceforth assume control of all aspects of development and preparation. Two dynos were installed by the end of 1992.

It should be stressed that engine building was not a source of conflict with STi. The partnership between the two firms was if anything strengthened as a result and Moore's enthusiasm is unconcealed when he recalls the arrival of another STi engineer, Matsurai Kurihara.

As development advanced, the Legacy's standard origins became more of a drawback. The electronics and the induction system figured prominently in this respect. Unlike most of its rivals, the Legacy retained an airflow meter, which rarely came off best in an encounter with a muddy puddle. Dispensing with it hadn't been an option until Kurihara, a software engineer, arrived with a programme that functioned without the meter.

'It was so difficult, the early engine management system. It was a road car system and it was just extremely time consuming. Everything was in hexadecimal, so you had to hand-type in every address into the EPROMs [Erasable Programmable Read-Only Memory chips], and I wouldn't like to hazard a guess as to how many thousands of numbers you had to type in manually, but it was that bad. It used to take an eternity to do it, to change the settings on the engine. But when this guy came over – Kurihara-san – with the new software, it was like Christmas,' Moore recalled.

It was such an improvement that the team gambled on fitting it to one of the 1992 RAC cars. Later, Moore was sent to Japan for training in the software code. Laptop tuning had arrived.

It was an instance of the partnership's effectiveness and the growing confidence between the two sides. Richards recalled that the rally programme had already had another useful benefit.

'One of the early things we did was when they had trouble recruiting high-quality engineers and they were looking to target engineers from Tokyo University. We went out there with Markku Alén and a rally car on their test track and we hosted a day for the brightest young engineers from Tokyo University. FHI and Subaru was not perceived in those days as being an ambitious young company which modern engineering students would wish to join, but we soon changed that perception.'

The 1993 season also marked the beginning of a lengthy relationship with British American Tobacco and its 555 brand. It led to the launch of a serious bid for the Asia-Pacific Championship, as China was the largest market for 555 cigarettes, but it also demonstrated to Subaru that other companies were taking its efforts seriously. It had another effect too. The mechanics had been horrified to learn that pink was Subaru's official colour, blended for clothing purposes with trousers on the orange side of beige. 555's livery was dark blue with yellow signwriting. It proved so popular and so closely identified with the sponsor that they have become Subaru's official colours.

As it neared its peak, the Legacy entered the twilight phase of its competition career, with the Impreza taking shape in the wings. In fact, the two cars were rallied in parallel for several months: there was no apparent rush to bring the replacement into action, and frankly no pressing need. In July 1993, McRae finally achieved Subaru's first victory on a World Championship rally and the first for a British driver since 1976, withstanding intense pressure from François Delecour's Escort Cosworth to take the Rally of New Zealand. The foundations for a World Championship assault had been laid.

Content that the Legacy had proved its worth, STi duly authorised the switch to the Impreza.

Both team and driver were at home in the conditions, but Colin McRae's 1993 New Zealand triumph was in doubt until the finish was almost in sight, when he finally shook off François Delecour's Escort.

2 The car that
created the legend

Racing car designers have long been celebrated, from Ettore Bugatti to Colin Chapman, Gordon Murray to Mauro Forghieri. Any well-informed Grand Prix fan would recognise Ross Brawn, Patrick Head and Adrian Newey.

Rallying is somewhat different, not least because, aside from the fleeting period when Group B was at its wildest, the engineer's role has been not to create a car from scratch, but to modify a road car for a specific purpose. The rally engineer isn't a designer in the same sense. In so far as the Impreza 555 was the creation of one man, the credit goes to Hideshige Gomi, who led the design team in Japan. Prodrive's involvement was peripheral.

Yet the rally engineer can still stamp his personality on a car, and Prodrive's Subarus have long owed a great deal to David Lapworth, the team's original engineer. The early cars in particular blended innovation and practicality. They were and remain adventurous. Subaru has a fine record on rugged events such as the Acropolis and the Safari, yet Lapworth and his successors have never been content to win rallies on reliability alone.

Lapworth is fascinated by almost any form of motorsport with the possible exception of Formula 1 and would spend more time on trials bikes if the job permitted, but among rally engineers he has had few equals. Born in Coventry in 1956, the son of a trade union official who had worked for Morris Engines, he had talked his way from Talbot's engineering scheme to a job in the Competitions Department working for Des

O'Dell within weeks of graduating from a course at Leeds University and Lanchester Polytechnic. He was 22. At the time, four-wheel drive was for Land Rovers, and turbocharging was a weird technology pursued in rallying by Saab alone.

Some rally engineers admit that they have mixed feelings about their environment. Compared to racing, there are far too many unpredictable factors, from the sheer length of the route to the weather. It's impossible to map an entire rally electronically; from a scientific perspective, it is inherently untidy. To Lapworth, that's part of the appeal.

'What you try to do is build up the knowledge to be able to predict those things, but there is still an element of intuition, or whatever you want to call it. You rely a lot on the driver's feedback as well. You can't just look at the data and tell if the car's easy to drive. You can maybe evaluate certain characteristics, but it's only the driver who can tell you whether the feeling's right. Only he can really predict how well he will be able to drive it on a rally. We can measure theoretically it will go round this corner x-per cent better and so on, but it's still quite difficult to extrapolate that to rally conditions. I think that adds to the interest in rallying. From an engineer's point of view – from my point of view anyway – it's nice to think that there are still aspects of the job that haven't been quantified,' he said.

He has an enquiring mind, a taste for unconventional thinking (colleagues have been known to suggest that he is occasionally 'away with the fairies') and a competitive instinct, but he is no perfectionist. In a

The Impreza's potential was obvious the moment it appeared. Ari Vatanen led fleetingly and finished a close second on the 1993 1000 Lakes.

competitive environment, perfection takes too long to attain.

The transfer from Sunbeam Lotus to Peugeot 205 T16 placed the emphasis on Peugeot, not Talbot, and the shift in power from Britain to France left him without a full-time job at the end of 1983. He was working for himself, building Samba engines at home in Coventry, and filling in with the Carlisle tuner, Mike Little, who was running a Samba for Andrew Wood, when the chance to join Prodrive came. Since 1996, when David Richards first became involved in Formula 1 with Benetton, Lapworth has been a manager as much as an engineer and he hasn't had a direct role in designing rally cars since the late 1990s. His influence naturally endures and while it has become a sizeable organisation, the idea of Prodrive without him is inconceivable.

An easy-going, engaging man without a trace of conceit, he is good company, cheerfully prepared to discuss the notional effectiveness of Hydragas suspension on a rally car or to fly economy, sometimes both

at once. He has made a fine ambassador for Subaru and Prodrive.

The Impreza 555 was very much Lapworth's car. There were no half measures, no doubts within Subaru or Prodrive about either side's ambitions or abilities. It was built to win, to do everything the Legacy did, but to do it better.

Size was the obvious difference. The Impreza was 170mm shorter and 15mm narrower, but the wheelbase was reduced by just 60mm. The new car was lighter and nimbler, with a smaller frontal area, a lower centre of gravity and a lower moment of inertia.

It became the first Subaru to inspire something akin to religious devotion, and yet there is a heretical view of the Impreza put forward by none other than McRae. He preferred the Legacy and has long argued that it would have been just as quick if it had had the same engine.

'The Legacy was a better car to drive. It was a better-balanced, more neutral car than the Impreza. The Impreza was more of a nervous, twitchier car,' he maintained.

The underbonnet layout closely resembled the Legacy's, the flat-four engine mounted low and longitudinally, with the intercooler laid flat just in front of the bulkhead.

McRae wouldn't intend that as a damning criticism of the Impreza – not when it made him World Champion – and it isn't a view that would be universally shared. Richard Burns, who first sampled an Impreza shortly before the 1993 RAC, recalls it rather differently.

'It was certainly quicker on the stage we were testing on than the Legacy was. It was just a sharper, more precise car, but quite a similar feeling to it. You could totally tell it was virtually the same car under the skin when you got in it and the way it felt. It handled quite similar, but just more precise, direct – just a short, just a chopped Legacy – less likely to swipe the boot off it.

'I think those Legacys Alister [McRae] and I had in the RAC were probably the nicest and quickest ones that ever came out, so with the Impreza being right at the beginning of its development, I don't know that it necessarily felt that special. I think it was just more the ability of it to be more manoeuvrable, more nimble. It seemed to get out of corners quicker. It maybe had better

traction just because of the compactness of it,' he said.

Lapworth, the high priest of Impreza design, wouldn't have much time for heresy.

'One man's response is another man's nervousness,' he argued, shortly before the car's first appearance in August 1993. 'A short-wheelbase car inherently has better response. It's more of a "race" car to drive: if you can maintain the driver's confidence, that's all positive. So far as we're concerned, everything is positive. Will the car be quite as stable over the biggest bumps and jumps? No, it won't be, but when the drivers come to the first tight corner, the fact that they can brake later and turn in absolutely at the theoretical right place rather than ten metres beforehand to account for the momentum, it's all positive.

'What's happening now is as it gets more competitive, the emphasis shifts away from being easy to drive to what is the limit. It always happens. Every time there's a radical change in the regulations, that's a process we go through all over again. In the early days,

In Group A, the interior's standard origins were undisguised. The most advanced feature, the gearchange paddles on the steering wheel, found little favour with the drivers.

while people haven't got their act together very well or while things are still developing, the emphasis tends to be on making it easy to drive and then, as it gets more and more competitive, they start taking the easy to drive for granted and then you start to concentrate more and more on response.

'When it gets to the crunch, we're getting to the stage now there isn't any room for the faint-hearted. It is down to the best six drivers in the world giving it everything they've got.'

The Impreza was accordingly Subaru's answer to the growing sophistication and competitiveness of Group A, seven years after it supplanted Group B. But McRae was right in highlighting another aspect: the cars were so closely related that many of the Impreza's improvements might have been incorporated in the older car.

As Riddle put it, 'The Impreza was our first proper go at rounding up all the problems. We'd sticky-taped and gone along with the Legacy, and as successive things broke, we'd fixed it. It was getting to the point of being reliable at the end of its days. But the Impreza was the first thing that you thought, "This is the right size car", and we put to bed a hell of a lot of our niggles all at once then.

'I think just the packaging of the whole thing we managed to do nicer and better. The bodywork would stay together. You know, the wiring loom and the interior were done properly rather than the first one. We've got an example of our first one over there now [in the museum] and you look inside and think, "My God! Did we used to do that, aluminium and anodised?" The first Impreza was done nice: the ECUs were all in the right place and properly fitted, and just packaged well I think is the best way to describe the car. It was a good car really.'

A majority of the parts would have swapped directly, including the engine, the gearbox and suspension. Not many did. When Lapworth and a small team that included Bob Farley, Ian Morton, Mick Metcalfe and Graham Moore began work in January 1993, they seized the opportunity to reconsider almost every aspect of the original design.

'There's lots of advantages you get just by being able to do the job all over again,' Lapworth explained. 'That is at least as important as anything else: we've been able to move tanks around, play with the weight distribution a bit, do a better job of all sorts of things. We've gone to a slightly better level on the diff control system; we've improved the data logging system on the car; we've got a new dashboard layout; we've been able to rationalise the wiring looms better; we've been able to introduce a new radiator that works slightly better, which we would have liked to have done with the Legacy, but it wasn't quite the right time and there was a new car coming along, new cooling fans – all sorts of little details that in themselves don't add up to anything, but the sum of 100 details is a significant improvement and on top of that, I suppose an extra 20 horsepower never did any harm.'

The engine was the biggest change. There were no significant modifications to the crankcase, the heavily oversquare 92 x 75mm bore and stroke being retained, but the cylinder heads, the turbo, the cooling system (the intercooler as well the radiator and fans) and the electronics were substantially altered.

The cylinder heads were new, with a narrower valve angle (reduced from 26 to 20.5 degrees) and conventional, bucket-type tappets in place of the Legacy's finger-type, which had had an occasional tendency to explode through the rocker covers at high revs. To Prodrive's delight, Subaru had specified a bigger turbocharger from IHI and fitted a larger, air-to-air intercooler, although it was still sited above the engine, laid flat and fed through a scoop on the bonnet, rather than fitted upright at the front. Turbo and intercooler were both critical factors in Group A, because both had to be standard and therefore fitted to at least 2,500 road cars, after the minimum production figure was reduced. The Legacy's turbo had grown larger during its production run, but it was always smaller and delivered appreciably less power than its main rivals. The revised engine not only gave substantially more power, but sustained it too.

The car was tested three times in wind tunnels. As Group A rules required standard bodywork, this wasn't solely to do with downforce, but cooling. Improving airflow through the engine bay helped maintain testbed power in the most arduous conditions, most notably on the Acropolis, which combined high ambient temperatures with low average speeds. Accordingly, the sump guard was shaped to assist under-bonnet aerodynamics as well as ward off rocks and ridges. Running temperatures were reduced by 5° Celsius.

Although the parts were interchangeable, a few millimetres of extra suspension travel were extracted, thanks partly to redesigned driveshafts. The electronics were also upgraded, still consisting of a mixture of hardware. The ECUs were supplied by FHI from Japan, while the London firm, GEMS,

was responsible for the data logger as well as assembly. However, the memory capacity was increased and reliability improved considerably, partly because sensitive equipment was enclosed in a more substantial container and partly thanks to the adoption of military connectors. Attempting to keep the interior of a rally car bone-dry is a fruitless task, and the best that can be expected is that it is stopped from turning into a bath. Consequently, the equipment needs to be as rugged as possible. Greater sophistication also led to the appearance of electricians on the Prodrive payroll rather than sub-contracting the design of the wiring loom.

This reflected the growing significance of electronics. The mandatory 38mm turbo restrictor was still much the biggest cap on performance, but processor capacity was beginning to tell. GEMS had produced a data logger with a screen for the Legacy, making it

Hostile conditions on the 1993 RAC caught out many drivers, Colin McRae included, but Ari Vatanen delivered another solid result, bringing his Impreza 555 home fifth.

easier to trace faults, but the Impreza required another advance, as Prodrive prepared to introduce an active front differential. Nonetheless, although the preparations were made and testing had commenced, the Impreza was a more conservative design when it went into action on the 1993 1000 Lakes than its engineers had originally planned. There had been a few engine failures in testing, in fact, thanks mainly to over-ambitious machining of the piston crowns, but the Legacy had gone so well in its Indian summer that the team decided to defer some of the more radical features of its successor.

The active front and rear differentials were kept in reserve, although both were promised for 1994. Lapworth hinted too that active suspension was under consideration.

Nevertheless, at a time when some Formula 1 cars still had manual gearchanges, Subaru went to Finland with semi-automatic gearboxes. It wasn't the first team to explore such technology (Lancia had dabbled with a two-pedal Valeo system on Delta Integrales) but it was the first to fit it routinely to all its cars.

The system was pneumatically operated and relied on paddles on the steering wheel to change up and down. The clutch and gear lever remained – the gear lever moved through its usual H-pattern when the paddles were operated, in fact – but the drivers had the option of making ultra-quick, failsafe changes. Prodrive had calculated that the quickest manual shifts took 0.12 seconds, whereas the semi-automatic was capable of switching ratios in 0.04 seconds. Engine inertia made 0.10 seconds a more practical figure, however.

Yet the semi-automatic shift remained a footnote. Not for the last time, Lapworth found that he was the victim of driver conservatism. It was all very well telling them

On the 1994 RAC, the vast crowds witnessed the result they had longed for: Colin McRae became the first British driver to win the event since 1976, comfortably outpacing his rivals in a convincing display of Subaru superiority.

that they had the capacity to make faster, flawless gearchanges, all without removing their hands from the steering wheel, but it was much harder to convince them that this would feel right when hurtling through a forest; McRae admitted that he used it solely – occasionally at that – on road sections.

McRae wasn't part of the line-up in Jyväskylä. Instead, Subaru called on two seasoned Finns who were more than familiar with the team and terrain, Alén and Vatanen. The notion of Finnish invincibility had been shattered by victories for Carlos Sainz and Didier Auriol in the preceding three years, but McRae's Legacy-crunching charge to eighth the previous year would have made him a very bold choice indeed for the new car's first appearance. Besides, the Finns had nine 1000 Lakes wins between them.

Yet the team was in trouble before the later numbers had even crossed the start ramp. Alén's blistering getaways on home ground were legendary. On this occasion, though, he didn't even last the first stage, his brand new Impreza ending up in the trees with mortal damage to the steering and the cooling system. With characteristic acidity, John Spiller suggested over the radio that Markku might care to leave his overalls in the forest. The mechanics could scarcely believe their ears.

Spiller's waspish humour had been in fine fettle but, sure enough, Alén was never summoned for active service again, although he was periodically called in for testing, notably for the Safari.

'I don't know what happened. It feel like normal, I start like normal – 110% – it start small accident and then it was big accident. Maybe I try too hard,' Alén reflected.

The pressure on Vatanen was redoubled, but gradually he began to gain the upper hand. As the second leg snaked its way back towards Jyväskylä, Auriol's challenge stuttered when he landed much too hard over a jump, damaging his Celica's oil cooler and front suspension, leaving Vatanen to confront the Frenchman's Toyota teammate, Juha Kankkunen. Following the collapse of his co-driver, Juha Piironen, with a stroke some

weeks previously, Kankkunen had resorted to Denis Giraudet as a stand-in; it was the first time the two had rallied together and the first time the Frenchman had read English pace notes. Kankkunen was therefore driving to some degree from memory.

As the tempo increased, it cannot have been comfortable being any of the top co-drivers, regardless of the language used. As the crews left the rest halt at Jämsa, the tide was running in Subaru's favour and on the 26th of the 35 stages, Vatanen nosed ahead of Kankkunen, who had led from the outset.

Then, as night fell, the team was undone by one of those aggravating faults that sometimes befall new cars. It turned out that the auxiliary lamp pods mounted on the bonnet had a hitherto undetected effect on the aerodynamics: instead of drawing air in, the bonnet scoop expelled it and thus the water-cooling spray for the intercooler. Temporarily unsighted and not sure where the demister switch was, Vatanen lost 15 seconds and the lead.

Kankkunen hadn't quite made his escape, but his 17-second margin that night was safe enough. Second place was ultimately a disappointment to Subaru, but it had provided ample cause for satisfaction too. Kankkunen became World Champion that year after all and, the lamp pods apart, the Impreza had more than fulfilled expectations. It had proved easy to drive, admirably stable and notably less demanding on its tyres than the Celica. Vatanen had promised that he hadn't had to take undue risks.

The Impreza was promptly sidelined, for good practical reasons. The team's next scheduled World Championship appearance was on the Rally Australia, which involved a different set of equipment. Given the sheer tonnage of cars and spares involved, airfreight was prohibitively expensive and, in common with other rally teams, Subaru had European and non-European service vehicles, spares and cars. Switching to the new car in mid-season would have invited trouble and the old warhorse therefore made its final World Championship appearance in Perth, Vatanen and Bruno Berglund finishing second to the flying Kankkunen after McRae, to his undisguised disgust, beached his Legacy on the inside of a bend on the final day and plunged from second to sixth.

It was not a result to savour in any sense: Bourne had left the road at high speed early in the rally and landed in the trees. He was unhurt, but his irrepressible co-driver, Rodger Freeth, the Auckland astrophysics professor and former motorcycle racer, died two hours later in hospital from massive internal injuries.

Back in Europe, the sense of anticipation surrounding the RAC Rally bordered on the feverish. McRae had been quick enough to lead the event convincingly in a Legacy. Lombard had offered a £100,000 prize to any British driver who won the rally the year before. This time, noting McRae's growing stature and the arrival of the new Subaru, it was taking no such chances.

McRae didn't need a financial incentive and the further north the rally went, the more assured he looked. He hit his stride in Wales to spectacular effect, reeling in Kankkunen hand over fist and bursting into the lead on the 19th of the 35 stages. For once, he managed to get through Grizedale without mishap, but the rally was settled in the snowy wastes of Kielder.

McRae succumbed to the forest's first and most westerly stage, Kershope. It's a notoriously awkward test and somehow a branch or a log found its way into the radiator. The Impreza duly completed the stage, but a death rattle had set in. Although it ran again, briefly, it was beyond help. Subaru made do with fifth from Vatanen and departed with an abiding sense of unfinished business, while Kankkunen romped to victory and the world title.

The 1993 forays had been ranging shots. 1994 brought a new level of commitment. For the first time, Subaru contested the World Championship in full. It wasn't an exercise in gaining experience or making a splash in key markets, but an uncompromising assault, involving three Imprezas on some events – and an Asia-Pacific programme on top.

To do so, it recruited an undisputed number-one driver, Sainz. Very occasionally, a car is so superior that the driver ceases to matter very much, but as a rule he plays the pivotal role and Sainz marched Subaru to new heights. Alén and Vatanen were illustrious figures, but both were in their 40s and past their zenith, while at 25, McRae wasn't quite the finished article. Sainz, then 31, had established himself as one of the supreme all-rounders by winning rallies as different as the Monte Carlo, the Safari and the 1000 Lakes. He had a formidable reputation as a test driver and also possessed a devoted following in Spain that made him a magnet to sponsors. The oil company, Repsol, promptly joined 555 as one of the team's backers.

It is difficult to overstate his influence. As Richards observed: 'Carlos, I would say, was one of the key people that galvanised the team, because there was no denying his work ethic and his professionalism, and he came along at a time when things were starting to come together very well. Some drivers sit back and say, "My job is to drive the motor car, their job is to run the team and run the test programme." Carlos wanted to be involved in everything. He would want to be involved in all the testing, he would be the last one there on a test session, he would be the one who pushed Pirelli to get the tyres right for us, he would be the one that drove everybody just that little bit harder, just to get the best out of things.'

Mechanics recall that when dealing with Sainz, there was no place to hide.

'Carlos brought determination, a very particular sort of attitude,' Riddle explained. 'I can't quite think of the word that describes how he is, but he knows what he wants and he doesn't stop until he gets it; different to our previous drivers. He thought more about it, I think. All our drivers up until then, like Markku and Colin and Ari – Marc Duez – had all been "feel" drivers. They would tell you when a wheel was missing, but they wouldn't be able to tell you when there was one just slightly out of bed, whereas Carlos could. He wasn't always right, but he was

much more particular and his drive made sure that you paid much more attention to it.

'He absolutely made sure that if he wanted something done, he got it done. We wouldn't have become a championship-winning team without a guy of his make-up and his experience. He was the first guy we had who was categorically equal favourite every time you went out, and that really made us have to think every time we went out.'

In addition, Sainz brought recent technical knowledge from other teams. This also proved invaluable.

Subaru took another strategic decision at the same time, switching from Michelin to Pirelli. Picking any tyre maker other than these two would have been lunacy, but choosing between the two was not easy. Prodrive had worked successfully with both, but there had been a tendency for Pirelli users to transfer contentedly to Michelin rather than the other way round. The calculation in making the opposite move was that the Milanese firm was smaller and

therefore more responsive. It could develop new tyres substantially faster than Michelin, not least because it had fewer manufacturers to supply. Its ability to mix compounds that worked in cold, damp conditions inspired the thought that it employed sorcerers, not chemists, and for 1994 it was promising an answer to Michelin's run-flat ATS system. EMI (an abbreviation for Expanded Moduling Insert) uses a sealant mounted on the wheel that inflates to fill the tyre if it punctures, and it made its first appearance on the 1994 Rally of Portugal. It adds around 3.5 kilos to each wheel, but the ability to complete stages on punctures at undiminished speed made it worth its weight in gold.

By Portugal in March, the Impreza's failings had become all too apparent. Tarmac testing hadn't started until the previous September, after its Finnish appearance, and the cars were some way off the pace on a largely dry Monte; Sainz was third, McRae tenth, after losing a good deal of time when

In New Zealand in 1995, his opponents expected a drubbing and McRae confirmed their worst fears. Another masterly assault on the legendary Motu Road put him in the clear and on his way to a hat-trick.

he went off on snow thrown on the road by spectators.

The same weakness hampered both drivers on the opening, asphalt leg in Portugal; play in the front wheel bearings causing pad knock-off. Sainz finished fourth, while McRae's car went up in flames.

By the third round, the Tour of Corsica, the Impreza's Tarmac performance had been improved to such effect that only a freakish failure in the last leg demoted Sainz to second. After three days, he had finally settled on a satisfactory braking compromise by combining hard Corsican with softer Portuguese pads in the front calipers and looked to have gained the measure of Auriol, whose Toyota was slowed a little by a faulty oil seal. Then, the Subaru's front anti-roll bar snapped at the critical moment and Auriol made sure of a fifth island victory by a whisker over a minute.

Most of the improvement had been achieved by adjusting transmission settings, and part of the secret had been using the long-promised active front differential. It wasn't fitted during the rally, but it proved its worth in testing. The slip-limiting characteristics of an active, hydraulic differential can be altered swiftly by reprogramming the electronics, a considerably faster process than the laborious business of trying an assortment of mechanically operated differentials with different clutches and ramps. Once a satisfactory setting with the active unit was found, the team did its best to reproduce the characteristics with the mechanical, clutch-type differential.

Loose surfaces had posed few difficulties. Almost any driver down the years would echo Sainz's view, but his authoritative summary confirmed that the Impreza was as good as the team had hoped.

'The Subaru was nice car, nice handling, low centre of gravity already, good, comfortable, very good turning in, nice engine – not exceptional – but nice engine, from the bottom it was pulling very nicely. It was good turn-in I would say was the main thing, and the other thing was very good as

well was due to the boxer engine, you have very good clearance. That is something people never talk about, but it is such an important thing in rallying that allows you to go quite low in ride height, in gravel especially. That allows you to move the sump and the protection quite high and that is very important advantage I think in the Subaru,' he said.

Innovation on the Acropolis was always liable to end in tears, but as Sainz demonstrated, Prodrive didn't need it anyway. By the halfway point, the Imprezas had cut the opposition to shreds. In places, Sainz and McRae arrived ten minutes in advance, yet started the stage before another car had even come into sight. Sainz fulfilled the potential that the car had first displayed the previous August with a resounding victory, yet the rally had been plain sailing for neither team nor driver.

For much of the distance the winner trailed the upstart McRae. Indeed, the Scot looked more likely to take the Impreza's first victory until a bad-tempered clash with officialdom. The scrutineers carried out a spot check at a regroup in Makrakomi, a village on the main road west of Lamia, but inadvertently failed to refasten the bonnet pins. McRae found out within a few hundred yards of the time control when the bonnet flew open and smashed the windscreen. There wasn't enough service time to replace the windscreen without incurring road penalties and, on the basis that officials had caused the problem, he demanded to be allowed to change it penalty-free at the next stage start.

The rally was delayed for half an hour while this request was considered, then granted. Later that afternoon, Sainz pounced when McRae nudged a rock and damaged a wheel bearing, but the windscreen affair hadn't ended. McRae was excluded by the stewards that evening for allegedly blocking the road and preventing other cars from starting the stage; a charge that he denied.

By New Zealand, the McRae Question had erupted again and there were rumours that his next accident would be his last on

Subaru's payroll. His first visit to Argentina had also ended badly, when a volley of fastest stage times was cut short by an encounter with a stone on the outside of a fast corner that tightened more than he had realised in the recce. It would have been bad enough if it had ended there, but to Richards's fury, his never-say-die Scot dragged the car another ten miles on three wheels until the sump, sump-guard and engine gave up the ghost. He had finished only once all season (there had been another accident in Corsica) and scored precisely one World Championship point.

Richards has admitted that he was periodically put under pressure by sponsors and by Subaru to get rid of McRae. Some of the more damning public pronouncements were thus intended partly for internal consumption. Putting some of the threats into practice must have been tempting, especially when his results were compared to Sainz's, but McRae's raw talent was simply too great to cast aside in exasperation.

Asked if McRae responded best to threats, he replied, 'I've tried everything, as one does. One tries mothering him and loving him and saying how great you are, and then if that doesn't work, you go to the other extreme, you say, "What a twit you are. What have you been doing here? Just use your head."'

From inside the car, it never seemed as wild as it sometimes did from the outside. Derek Ringer, who had been McRae's co-driver since his early days in the Scottish Championship, had no doubt about his driver's capabilities.

'Once you've sat in the car with him, then you realise just how much balance and natural ability – he's just in control. I know it doesn't look that way from the outside. The whole thing seems so easy – and you get used to the speed after a while!

'It depends how much you feel he actually needs to be controlled. I don't think that's a very fair term to use. I mean, we're not talking about a kid or something like that and it's the easiest thing in the world to say after the accident's happened, "You should have told him to go slower." It doesn't quite

work like that. You're in control until the moment you've had the accident.'

At the time, the World Championship for Manufacturers was decided counting the score of the make's highest-placed car on each rally, and Sainz didn't seem to need much assistance in any case. In one of the most memorable Rallies of Argentina, he swapped the lead with Auriol no fewer than

The transmission was one of the keys to the Impreza 555's success. Prodrive and Subaru were months, and in some cases years, in front of their rivals in developing active differentials.

11 times. The two were never separated by more than 20 seconds throughout. The Spaniard's Subaru was slowed once by power-steering failure, and twice by faulty EMI inserts that set up a chronic vibration. Auriol fended Sainz off by all of six seconds. The Toyota men were generous enough to describe the outcome as a draw.

Most teams would have thought twice before introducing a major modification for a rally on the far side of the globe, but Prodrive was coming to regard New Zealand as a home from home, and Lapworth was confident that the next advance in active transmission technology was ready. Active control would be extended to the front. While the centre differential is generally accepted as playing the biggest part in dictating the behaviour of a four-wheel-drive system, the front differential's effect on the steering makes it crucial. Lapworth was seeking a new answer to the 'unavoidable equation', that a tighter differential means better traction, but tends to make the car steer disconcertingly as well.

'There are times when a conventional diff will be tighter than you need it to be,' he explained. 'Now, by having a more sophisticated control system, when it doesn't need to be tight, it doesn't need to be, does it? That's the problem you have at the moment: you choose a diff for the worst situation and it's there when you don't need it. It's there when you're accelerating down a straight in sixth gear and it's not necessary then. You need the traction when you come out of a slow corner in first.'

McRae readily confirmed its effectiveness and that the weight penalty of seven to eight kilos was well worthwhile.

'First of all, the centre diff and then the active front diff made a big difference to the car. It just meant the car was more controllable in longer corners and bad cambers. The problem with the old mechanical diffs was that you could spin the car very easily. It would lift a front wheel and then you would have no drive at all, but if it lifts a front wheel with an active diff, you've still got the active part driving the wheel and it pulls the car again,' he said.

Appropriately enough, Carlos Sainz's final win for Subaru was taken in front of his adoring fans, but there was nothing straightforward about his victory in Catalonia.

But it wasn't McRae who was expected to demonstrate its worth. After a run of dire results and a severe warning, he suggested that he would be content with fifth. Sure enough, Sainz led at first, only for his engine to blow up within hours of the start. Subaru had taken control, nonetheless, by the end of the leg. The car fulfilled every expectation and McRae, who knew the terrain better than almost any other World Championship rally, led almost in spite of himself. Car and driver were in a different league and the rally was as good as settled at half distance after the Motu Road, the longest, twistiest and least forgiving stage of the rally. 'Motu-meister', proclaimed the exuberant headline in *Motoring News*.

It was a turning point. Sainz drove the solitary works entry to third place on the 1000 Lakes (it had been decided not to send McRae before his New Zealand triumph), but the Scot followed that with a victory in Australia. It wasn't part of the full World Championship that year, taking its turn as a two-wheel-drive championship round thanks to the much-derided rotation system then in use, under which every rally dropped a rung down the ladder for one year in three. However, Toyota had regardless sent Kankkunen to step up development of the new Celica GT-Four. The Finn had lost the event only once since it had been introduced to the World Championship. McRae held him off to win by nine seconds.

McRae drove impressively on the Sanremo Rally, too, taking fifth and outpacing Sainz during the final leg on the sinuous asphalt roads in the Ligurian mountains, which Sainz knew like the back of his hand. The Spaniard finished a close, but disappointing second. The pressure was beginning to tell: only Sainz and Auriol were still in the running for the World Championship, and after the first stage Auriol was ready to give up, declaring that the front differential was broken and that his Toyota was undriveable. The engineers, sure that nothing was wrong, coaxed him back into the cockpit with some difficulty. By the last leg, he was back in contention, but almost too ill to stand,

At the time, second place was a bitter disappointment, but Colin McRae's ability to match Sainz in Catalonia was proof of his all-round capabilities and a vital step on his way to the world title.

whereupon Sainz froze and his adversary gained a priceless victory.

It would be settled on the RAC. Circumstances put team management as well as drivers under pressure. It made for an enthralling, but sometimes ill-humoured rally. Auriol was lucky to see the end of the first-leg tour of stately homes and race tracks after his co-driver, Bernard Occelli, misread a pace note and they careered into a rock at Chatsworth, which broke the steering.

At the head of the field, McRae had assumed control, with Sainz second. Auriol clawed his way back into a respectable position, giving Toyota the option of slowing its remaining drivers and promoting him to third. If he finished third, Subaru would need to order McRae to hand victory to Sainz to deprive Auriol of the World Championship.

To Sainz, well-used to team orders with other manufacturers – usually as the beneficiary, it must be said – it was the obvious solution. To the team, multi-national, working for the Japanese, but overwhelmingly British, it was too awful to contemplate. Richards maintained that it would be unsportsmanlike if Toyota shuffled the order and obliged him to follow suit.

The order never came. Instead, on a soggy, misty morning in Wales, a log unaccountably found its way on to the track in front of Sainz in Pantperthog. He missed it, but couldn't dismiss it as readily. On the following stage he slithered helplessly into a ditch. Spectators rushed to his assistance, but the car took an age to free. Sainz retired and to national rejoicing, the rally went to McRae, who trounced Kankkunen. But the championships went to Auriol and Toyota.

There was barely pause for breath. The Asia-Pacific season concluded ten days later in Thailand and, by then, preparations for the Monte and a distinctly different challenge in 1995 were well underway. The FIA had changed the points-scoring system, requiring that each registered manufacturer entered three cars per rally, counting the scores of the best two. Subaru therefore needed extra drivers and relied primarily on three new recruits, Richard Burns – McRae's successor

as British Champion, even younger and also highly promising – and a pair of more seasoned campaigners, Bourne and the Italian, Piero Liatti. He had been European Champion in 1991 in a Lancia and had latterly distinguished himself driving Legacys for the Modena-based team run by the Alessandrini brothers, Paolo and Alessandro.

There were new technical challenges too. To cut speeds and to ease the potentially disruptive effects of restricted servicing between stages, the FIA had banned slick tyres. All cars would be required to use moulded tyres at all times on World Championship rallies. It would be a shade misleading to describe the tyres used on dry Tarmac as treaded in the road car sense – a series of 'chicken-foot' markings merely ensured they complied with the requirement that a minimum of 17% of the tyre had a tread pattern – but there was an overnight fall in cornering speeds; the drivers were unappreciative.

They were, though, positively disgusted by the new engine rules, which reduced the turbo intake from 38 to 34 millimetres. A change had been anticipated, but the assumption had been that it would be to 36mm, much as the original 40mm restrictor had been reduced to 38. The 1995 ruling was not only a more severe reduction than anticipated, but much greater than it sounds, because the intake area is measured on a logarithmic scale.

Even co-drivers were unimpressed.

'It seemed that any corner faster than about third gear, Richard just couldn't slide the car,' Robert Reid observed. 'It wasn't the nicest thing to be in. I think the engine response and power have both got better, but certainly at that point it wasn't very pleasant. You ended up going off on the inside of corners all the time: it just ran out of grunt halfway through and nosedived off the inside.'

The power reduction was officially reckoned to be in the order of 15–20%, which amounted to approximately 50bhp, giving a true output of around 320–330bhp. The drivers – no matter which team they drove for – were agreed that it made controlling the cars more difficult at high speeds, but Subaru didn't fare as badly as some of its rivals, despite the Impreza's oversquare engine, which might have been expected to suffer badly from a reduction in maximum revs. In fact, the engine would still reach 8,000rpm, but there was no real benefit beyond 6,000rpm. Despite four valves per cylinder, advanced materials and highly sophisticated electronics, the new breed of rally engine had a lower effective rev limit than an all-iron, pushrod A-series had had in a Cooper S 30 years previously.

The EJ20's design did something to mitigate the effects. Its lightweight construction and short stroke reduced friction, which became a much more serious concern, and in any case, its IHI turbo had never taken full advantage of the possibilities offered by the 38mm restrictor. It worked quite well with the new limit. Besides, Prodrive had prepared thoroughly. Development with the smaller restrictor had begun in the summer and Sainz had appeared on the Catalonia Rally as a course car to gain experience. The new power curve, which ran from around 3,500–6,000rpm, demanded new camshafts with less overlap and the altered characteristics affected the transmission too. A lower rev range required longer gearing to reach the same maximum speed.

Development has since extended the power curve, but by starting it as low as 2,500rpm. At those revs, an Impreza can give up to three bar of boost, tailing off to half a bar at high revs. Tireless experimentation with restrictor shape has brought improvements of fractions of a per cent, while turbos have grown lighter and compression ratios have inched upwards, but as Lapworth concedes, the restrictor remains a highly effective device.

The groundwork had been laid, yet the team endured a nightmarish week on the Swedish, usually one of its best rallies. The double winner and local hero Mats Jonsson was drafted in to bolster the attack, to no effect. Unusually, the coating flaked off the

cylinder liners and jammed the oil pumps. It wasn't apparent when the engines were hot, but when they were cold it led to a colossal increase in oil pressure that blew the filters off. None of the three cars went the distance.

On almost every other rally, the Imprezas were in a class of their own. Sainz romped to a conclusive victory on the Monte – the rally

The driving force in the partnership between Subaru and Prodrive, David Richards was very much the architect of their earlier World Championship successes.

every manufacturer wants to win – and again in Portugal. He and McRae made do with fourth and fifth respectively in Corsica, and McRae settled for second in Australia, but it says something about the team's growing assurance that second place was a disappointment. Toyota was in disarray as it sought to cope with the 34mm restrictor and the new Celica's ungainly handling, Mitsubishi showed flashes of promise, but won only in Sweden and Australia, while Ford – well behind in developing active transmission – simply floundered.

'At that time, the team was emerging, the team was very motivated, everybody pulling the same direction. Technically it was very well and very well organised. Obviously, winning Monte Carlo was very nice, but for me the best probably was we were working all together to make the best car of the time. I enjoyed very much working with Lapworth and Christian Loriaux,' Sainz summarised.

Winning wasn't an entirely straightforward business, however. In early July, when leading the championship, Sainz had a bad mountain bike accident outside Madrid. It was the sort of mishap that might have been expected to befall the fearless McRae. Instead, the professional's professional was grounded by a broken collar bone. Burns was given a run in New Zealand in his place and while Sainz was back in harness for Australia in September, he wasn't fully fit and made an early exit thanks to a branch that holed the radiator and led to engine failure.

But McRae was looking ominously assured in any case. The opposition had known what to expect in New Zealand and, as they prepared to head to the Motu Road, the Toyota drivers freely admitted that they expected to lose a minute. They were right, and McRae completed a hat-trick without appearing to extend himself.

In an eight-round championship, the Celica men retained a mathematical chance of stealing the title as late as the penultimate round, but they had been reduced to outsiders. Subaru's success was storing up its own problems, though, and in front of Sainz's home crowd in Catalonia, the storm burst.

It was one of the most bitterly contested rallies in World Championship history and the outcome will remain controversial long after the protagonists are old and grey. For much of the event, the Imprezas trailed Kankkunen, who was putting in an unusually strong showing on asphalt, but when the Finn crashed towards the end of the penultimate leg, the Subarus were unopposed, Sainz leading by a narrow margin from McRae, while Liatti was an assured third. With the drivers' and manufacturers' championships at stake, the question of team orders naturally arose. There was no need to jeopardise such a strong position, and after several hours, during which orders were issued, denied and confirmed, Richards disclosed that he had told his drivers to hold station, finishing in the order in which they completed the second leg: Sainz, McRae, Liatti.

To any true fan, team orders are unattractive; to some, they're unsporting; to any experienced observer, they are unlovely, yet routine. But to McRae, the decision was unbearable. He wasn't the first rising star to rebel and he had more reason than most, for it wasn't a mere rally at stake, but the World Championship. If he won, the 20 points would give him a ten-point lead over Sainz on the RAC. If he meekly finished second, they would start the RAC level.

It was too much to take and, just as Tommi Mäkinen had flouted Mitsubishi orders on the Swedish that year, McRae burst ahead of Sainz to take the lead. Richards had no intention of backing down. Indeed, he couldn't afford to be seen to back down. Spiller and Riddle were sent to the final stage to slow McRae and were forced to leap for safety as he scudded past, accelerator buried to the bulkhead. On stage times, McRae was the winner.

The team always wins. Once the car was in service on the main street in Lloret de Mar, only a few hundred yards from the finish ramp, but jacked up and minus its wheels, McRae had lost control. After a prolonged, tortured argument with Richards in one of the trucks, he took a minute's road penalty. The designated order was restored.

Sainz was outraged, partly that he had been exposed to ridicule at home, partly that it had been made to look as though he would not have won the rally on merit when he had driven the final leg with something in hand. He resents still that it is regularly claimed that he inherited victory.

His differences with McRae were patched up within days, before the showdown in Britain. It's unlikely that any of the Toyota drivers could have stood in the way, but the rally and the championship became a duel between the two even before the start. Post-event scrutineering in Spain revealed that Auriol's Celica was fitted with an illegal, adjustable turbo restrictor that permitted a substantial increase in power. The team and drivers were excluded not just from the rally, but the championship, and banned for the following 12 months.

Sainz was entitled to hope. He had won the RAC twice, Mäkinen's early lead ended

with an accident in Hamsterley and while McRae rocketed ahead in the County Durham forest he dropped over two minutes changing a puncture on the rally's longest stage in Kielder; he still averaged 65mph. Fighting back, he all but wrecked the front suspension when he slithered off in Kershope. But he survived. A mixture of brute force, experience and a convenient log helped straighten his Impreza enough for the run to service; and in Wales, Sainz was flattened.

He offered no excuses: there was nothing wrong with the car; he was given everything he wanted. It was just that there was no containing McRae. Running on a blend of ambition and adrenalin, the Lanark man managed to overturn the one-minute advantage his teammate had held after Kielder with a day in hand. It was an epic, yet somehow nonchalant performance; in the final leg he had even strolled into the pub in Corris for a game of snooker to pass the time before the first stage. The duel had turned

Following the arguments, the celebrations. Carlos Sainz and Luis Moya spray the champagne after winning the 1995 Catalonia Rally.

into a rout. McRae became the first British and the youngest ever World Rally Champion, Subaru gained the World Championship for Manufacturers for the first time and, to underline the Impreza's superiority, the team swept the top three places for the second rally in succession, Burns playing the part that Liatti had taken in Spain.

Along with his first victory in New Zealand, it is naturally McRae's fondest memory of his years with Subaru, and that view is shared by most of the older hands. There was nothing to beat 'the motley crew from Banbury' – Riddle's self-deprecating description of the band who had sallied forth with the Legacy in 1990. They had exceeded their wildest expectations.

It was a landmark for Subaru too. One of Japan's smaller car makers, it had beaten Mitsubishi and the leviathan Toyota. It was only the second time a Japanese manufacturer had won the World Rally Championship. Subaru's stature was no longer in question.

Sainz had originally planned to revert to Toyota, and when its 12-month ban made that impossible, he joined Ford instead. In his eyes, Subaru had become McRae's team.

'At the end, I felt I was probably not understanding very well and not staying together very well with some parts, and I decided for me driving is important, but driving in a happy way is also important and that time was not a happy time,' he explained.

Richards subsequently offered a marginally different perspective on McRae's relationship with the team.

'For all his failings, there's a great motivation for him in the team. The team rate him, the team know him very well and they've watched him grow up, and I think there's almost a feeling of shared destiny.'

Sainz's demanding yet steadying influence was not easily replaced. Perhaps the party was bound to be followed by a hangover. Perhaps it was too much to expect that the team could operate at the same pitch in 1996. Certainly, running four cars, as it did

Subaru at its zenith: in November 1995, a dominant performance in Catalonia enabled the Imprezas to sweep the first three places on a World Championship rally for the first time.

on the Swedish, stretched resources. Above all, perhaps it was asking too much of McRae, especially when faced with an opponent as talented and single-minded as Mäkinen.

Subaru didn't lose in 1996. Thanks to McRae, to Liatti and to Kenneth Eriksson (who had been poached from Mitsubishi, in part to bolster Subaru's Asia-Pacific attack) it retained the World Championship for Manufacturers by a comfortable margin. Nevertheless, the abiding memory is that 1996 was Mäkinen's year, for he became the only driver to win more than half the World Championship rallies in a season and made sure of a nine-round championship with two rallies to spare.

McRae admitted that he didn't adapt well to the burden of expectation. Being the underdog number two was one thing, achieving the superhuman month in, month out was another. With hindsight, he ought at the very least to have prolonged the contest until the closing rounds. One of the oddities of the last year of the rotation system was that the Tarmac rallies were concentrated at the end of the season and it wasn't apparent until then that the Impreza remained markedly superior to the Lancer Evo III on asphalt, when the Mitsubishi's suspect rear suspension did nothing for the handling. Under pressure to score points, Mäkinen might have been vulnerable.

However, that hadn't been apparent in the spring and summer. Mäkinen stormed to a widely anticipated victory on the Swedish, then amazed his foes – and his friends, for that matter – by taking the Safari. It had been his first attempt, the first for Ralliart Europe and the first for Prodrive. The Impreza 555 didn't excel in Kenya, despite a brief but carefully planned development programme, which included a ten-day test with Alén in December 1995 and involved the development of tougher Bilstein struts with 51mm tubes and remote oil reservoirs. The Imprezas had the customary extra protection fitted to Safari cars, while the ride height was raised by 50mm and the gearing was lengthened. Despite the switch from petrol to Avgas (then routine in Kenya) Lapworth reflected with disdain that a Safari car was probably slower than the Impreza he had driven to Heathrow on his way to Kenya; at altitudes of 5,000 to 10,000 feet, he reckoned it gave no more than 250bhp.

The rear suspension proved fragile, McRae knocking a rear wheel awry at one point and finishing fourth, while the never-say-die Eriksson was second, despite a broken driveshaft, brake trouble and a bout of overheating when sawdust clogged the radiator on the Mau Escarpment.

McRae scored a brilliant victory on the Acropolis in June, withstanding intense pressure from Mäkinen in a sweltering, nerve-racking sprint for the line on the atrocious roads south of Itea. The organisers had conceded an extra service point at the last minute and allowed crews to carry two spare wheels. Even so, many drivers, Mäkinen included, were limping into service with front tyres shredded to the canvas. McRae took just one spare for the decisive stages, not wanting to upset the handling with the extra weight. He didn't even bother with it, preferring not to switch tyres and possibly upset the car's feel.

The extra service point did no harm, though. The leading Impreza had arrived with an ominous vibration from the propshaft. McRae wasn't at all sure that it would have held. The service crew did him proud, replacing it in a fraction under ten minutes.

The Acropolis was often one of Prodrive's best rallies, but there wasn't much else to celebrate. McRae had crashed heavily when leading by a handsome margin in Indonesia, leaving Liatti to claw his way to a close second behind Sainz's Escort, then crashed again in Argentina, crushing the camshaft drive in the impact. In Finland, he left the road in the early stages again, the car expiring on the road section after crabbing out of the stage.

But his behaviour in Argentina had brought him to the attention of officialdom. He had arrived at a service point with a broken rear crossmember after clouting a rock. It was a difficult part to change in a hurry and he was three minutes late when he headed for the time control, as spectators scattered in all directions. He knocked down three. While none were injured, the FIA summoned him to a tribunal in Paris and fined him US$75,000 – equivalent to around £50,000 at 1996 exchange rates.

After Finland, Richards had had enough. Co-drivers get a raw deal: they get none of the glory, their own mistakes are mercilessly highlighted and they can also be blamed for their drivers' failings. Prodrive management concluded that a change would be best and Ringer was told that he would be sacrificed at the end of the season and replaced by Nicky Grist, Kankkunen's navigator.

It made for a strained atmosphere in the closing months of the season. McRae put in a shockingly anonymous performance to take fourth in Australia, well behind the runner-up Eriksson, let alone Mäkinen. There was none of the usual flamboyance at Sanremo or in Catalonia, but he won both, making sure

that Subaru retained the manufacturers' championship. In an echo of the very different challenge posed by the Acropolis, both wins were a tribute to the chassis and the tyres. The ability to retain grip, whether on abrasive roads in Tarragona or when using a soft intermediate on slimy, leaf-strewn mountain passes above Sanremo, had made much of the difference.

It was the Impreza 555's parting shot as a works car. It had no vices. Drivers and mechanics have equally pleasant memories of it. It's an indication of its worth that in little more than three years, Prodrive built 63 of them.

As Steve Wilson – never a staff member, but long one of Prodrive's stalwarts – put it: 'Good car, the old Group A Impreza. You could just drive over stuff: strong as an ox, easy to fiddle with.'

It had won 11 World Championship rallies, but by the time McRae pipped Liatti in Catalonia, it looked obsolete. A few days earlier, Prodrive had revealed its replacement.

A generation passed between the late Roger Clark's 1972 RAC victory with Tony Mason and the next all-British success, for Colin McRae and Derek Ringer, but there was no generation divide in celebrating the Subaru driver's home triumphs.

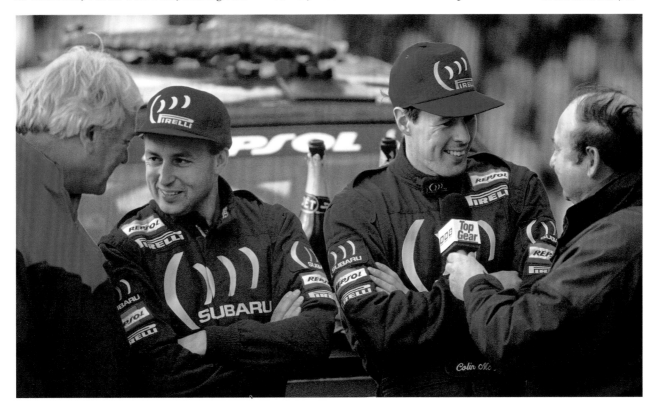

3 Cars with a Prodrive stamp

Take two otherwise identical cars, one of them painted blue, the other metallic blue and the solid blue one ought to be a fraction quicker. Metallic paint is heavier. But David Richards has long understood that appearances matter and the Impreza WRC97 was not only designed to take full advantage of the new regulations, but to live up to the old saying that if it looks right, it is right. The renowned designer Peter Stevens had been called in not simply to refine the aerodynamics, but to ensure that every detail, the interior included, reflected the fact that this was a new car for a new era. Retaining the World Championship was only part of the brief. The new machine was intended to capture the imagination. In essence, the Impreza WRC97 was a two-door version of the proven Impreza 555, but the range of modifications permitted meant that it amounted to a fresh design.

The FIA introduced a host of new regulations in 1997, governing both the rallies and the cars. The rotation system was abandoned and the World Championship was expanded from nine rallies to 14. In return, each event was shortened from 600 kilometres to a maximum of 400 kilometres (around 250 miles) of stages, with the exception of the Safari. While the rallies became true sprints, the steady reduction in service opportunities – to say nothing of the roads the Safari or the Acropolis organisers considered appropriate – ensured that reliability remained a prime virtue.

Group A continued, but it was supplemented by a new, related category. Every manufacturer other than Mitsubishi promptly switched to a World Rally Car. The new breed were genuine prototypes, more restrained in appearance yet further removed from the road car than even the Group B dragsters of the 1980s, but there was a critical difference: for the first time, the FIA had chosen to limit performance in rallying primarily by imposing a formula rather than a minimum production total.

The production link most certainly endured. A WR Car had to be derived from a 'family' of road cars made in minimum quantities of at least 25,000 per year. They had to be steel-bodied four-seaters, the basic engine had to be fitted to at least 2,500 road cars and it had to remain within 20 millimetres of its original position. However, there was no need to make a four-wheel-drive or turbocharged road version, and performance was limited by cubic capacity, turbocharger restrictor and intercooler size, suspension design, maximum width and maximum dimensions for aerodynamic devices. Eye-catchingly big aerofoils and flared wheel arches were allowed, but within prescribed limits. The floorpan could be cut open to fit a propshaft tunnel, rear driveline and bigger rear wheel arches, but the dimensions were defined and enforced. In summary, it was an attempt to solve the problems that Audi had originally posed when it unveiled the Quattro: that four-wheel drive had become essential, but that it was difficult and expensive to put into production, and that it risked setting off a dangerous escalation in performance.

For a manufacturer like Toyota, the new class presented an opportunity to fit much of

Win number one: Piero Liatti gave the first Impreza World Rally Car the perfect start, a superb victory on the Monte Carlo Rally.

the running gear from a Celica into the smaller Corolla bodyshell, even though the engine wasn't fitted to any showroom Corolla (limited concessions were soon made to the original regulations) and the sole four-wheel-drive variant was in no sense a performance car.

Subaru was in a very different position. An Impreza without four-wheel drive would be as unthinkable as a 911 without a rear-mounted flat-six, but the regulations offered sufficient freedom to make the WR Car option the obvious choice.

Subaru wanted to show that it was ahead of the game. The WRC97 was launched at a night club – all bass-driven music and spotlights – near Lloret on the eve of the 1996 Catalonia Rally, just a little before Ford unveiled a revamped Escort.

With a characteristic blend of enthusiasm and caution, David Lapworth confirmed that it didn't just look the part.

'I would say the aerodynamics have made a significant difference in the area where we feel we've been losing recently at high speed. It's more stable on asphalt. It's more stable from the width and the engine, we've got slightly more power and it's less temperature-sensitive. On a cold day on the RAC or in Sweden, there wouldn't be so much difference, but when it's hot, it should be better. What we believe is it's a significant enough improvement over what we've got. We wouldn't fear any of the cars now.'

The engine provided the best illustration of the scope of the new rules. Prodrive could have changed the bore and stroke had it wished, because the only restrictions on crankshafts and con rods were that they were specified on the homologation papers and the same design was used all season. There was some incentive to change, for Mitsubishi had demonstrated the formidable torque that could be extracted from a long-stroke layout when allied to the 34mm restrictor. However, there were also good practical reasons for leaving well alone. There wasn't much clearance between the flat-four's heads and the inner wings, and while lengthening the stroke was tempting, it wasn't worthwhile if

it made it impossible to change the sparking plugs.

Although turbochargers were free, provided they were specified and fitted with the restrictor, Prodrive retained the existing turbo. The regulations offered plenty of scope for increasing performance without taking chances, as Moore explained.

'I think the right thing was done. The first year of WR Cars, we didn't go silly with the turbocharger. We kept the turbo from the Group A car and obviously the mounting position was free. One of the restrictions of the Group A engine was we had to take the air under the inlet manifold, because that's the standard position for the turbocharger. But the WR Car, you have freedom of the exhaust system and we moved it, so you could get a massive increase. The biggest performance increase came from the massive air intake you could get on to the turbocharger: redesign the restrictor to get the best flow into it. Probably most of that came from the intake.

'The whole inner wing on the front left-hand side of the car was just the airbox. You've got a massive air filter, a big airflow, you get pressurised air round the headlight straight into the engine. You've got a massive increase – delivery of cold air was one of the biggest things you could get. And then, of course, the intercooler was huge. It was night and day,' he said.

The intercooler was repositioned too. The bonnet scoop is one of an Impreza's most distinctive features, but it has never had much of a practical role on a WR Car. The intercooler was placed vertically at the front above the radiator. Airflow through it was substantially improved and the old problem of heat soak from engine to intercooler was solved at a stroke.

A bigger turbo would have released more power, but risked creating problems of its own. It would have been another unknown quantity when there were already more than enough new features to address, and its extra mass would have impaired flexibility and throttle response. The alternative would have been to run a more aggressive anti-lag system. Thanks to electronics, these systems have become vastly more sophisticated since the 1980s, but in the Subaru's case, it still relied on running fuel through the cylinders on the overrun, effectively turning the turbo into a gas turbine to keep it spinning, so that power was available as soon as the driver accelerated again.

Moore always preferred a smaller turbo. More anti-lag led to a significant rise in exhaust valve and head temperatures.

'In the Subaru, the exhaust manifold is under the engine, so if you've got that at 1,000 degrees, the heat rises. You can put radiation shields on, but it's quite difficult. It's very easy to do an anti-lag strategy that will cook the engine. It's not so easy to do one that won't and still have the same response,' he said.

To improve the intake, the turbo was tipped to the maximum angle STi permitted, 20 degrees, and there was a complete redesign of the exhaust manifolds, which no longer had to be standard. The standard manifolds were siamesed and as short as possible, creating a Subaru's distinctive, uneven exhaust note; it has even given rise to the name of a magazine, *Boxer Sound*, in Japan. The sound changed, purely because of the new manifolds; Prodrive engineers unfailingly deny that they changed the firing order and insist that it remains one, three, two, four, firing each bank of cylinders in turn.

Freeing manifold design made it possible to fit equal-length manifolds and even out the firing pulses, but the objective was more easily stated than achieved. Prodrive toyed with the idea of installing the turbo centrally, but that would have raised the centre of gravity and the aim was to keep anything that hot as low as possible. Mounting the turbo to one side remained a pipe bender's nightmare.

'It's one of the hardest things, actually, in a flat four, the exhaust system, because you've got to carry it from the two other cylinders right across the turbo,' Moore said. 'The two

Win number two: Kenneth Eriksson rose to the occasion brilliantly on the Swedish to give the Impreza WRC97 its second victory.

Sub-zero conditions mean that tyres used on the Swedish are distinctly different from those used anywhere else; the angle of the tread blocks, the length of the studs and even the glue retaining them can make all the difference. In 1997, Pirelli did Subaru proud.

furthest from the turbo define the length you want and you effectively have twice tuned length, because you can't go tuned length – it's impossible – so you double it. So that's all right and then you think, "How am I going to get a metre of pipe in?" You curl it up as best you can. If you look at the exhaust manifolds on the early WR Cars, that's how they were: you've got all this big spaghetti junction round that side of the turbo.'

Prodrive considered altering the firing order, in fact, and even briefly contemplated following the route that Honda pursued in Grand Prix motorcycling by building a 'big bang' engine that fired two cylinders at once. Such ideas were discarded principally on the advice of Japan, which had carried out a good deal of experimentation on firing order at a much earlier stage in the flat-four's development and warned that all kinds of cam belt and crankshaft problems could arise.

The suspension followed well-established Subaru principles, with MacPherson struts all round, but the freedom to extend the width from the standard 1690mm to the regulation 1770mm brought a useful increase in suspension travel and, in theory at least, made it possible to optimise the geometry. One of the oddities of the WR Car formula is that while there is abundant scope for

altering rear suspension, the front continues to adhere to Group A, apart from the increase in overall width and therefore track. Mounting points may be moved no more than 20mm from their standard location and it follows that geometry must remain essentially similar.

There were no significant alterations to the transmission or the electronics for 1997. They were also considered to be well-proven areas that would suffice for the time being.

'The cage at the time was the very best that we knew how to do,' Riddle commented. 'It was a work of art and it was fundamental to the bodyshell, whereas in previous years the struts were where they came on the road car, give or take a little bit, and the roll cage joined up to them. It was a big, big step. I guess those World Rally Cars were the first ones that were specifically built to be rally cars. Everything else since Group B days had been an adaptation of what your manufacturer made, whereas people could go right back to the drawing board. It was a very successful car. It all just came together – there was no particular stroke of genius to it. We had good knowledge of how our car worked by then. We knew exactly how big or how heavy to make a trailing link or a lateral link and all that sort of stuff, so we were pretty confident that what was being done was right and, yeah, it worked sort of straight out of the box for us, really. And it looked beautiful as well – one of the cars that you could really say had a Prodrive stamp on it.'

This isn't boastful in the least, just a fair tribute to a superb car's record. It would be wrong to say that the World Championship for Manufacturers was over as a contest by the beginning of March, for it turned into a long and gruelling campaign, but it would be fair to say that by then, it had become a championship for Subaru to lose. The WRC97 proved its mettle with three straight wins, on rallies as different as the Monte, the Swedish and the Safari.

They were all successes to treasure: the Monte, which provided a good deal more rain than snow, was Liatti's sole World

Championship success, and richly deserved after McRae crashed; the pleasant Italian withstood ferocious pressure from Mäkinen before gaining the upper hand when the Finn came close to spinning over an enormous drop towards the end and slipped back to third.

There wasn't much snow on the Swedish either, the rally turning into a three-car dogfight, with Mäkinen making up ground fast after losing a minute through a gear selection problem. At the front, McRae exchanged seconds with Sainz and Eriksson, losing his chance of victory with a high-speed spin towards the end. Eriksson, who had carried out the bulk of the testing, ignored all the advice from the team and Pirelli for the last, critical stages, taking buffed ice tyres with shorter studs and romping home ahead of Sainz's Escort. The Swede regards it as the finest of his three wins on home ground.

It was a tribute to Prodrive and Pirelli thoroughness too. Well aware that keeping the studs in the tyres had proved a problem in previous years, testing for the Swedish had begun the previous summer, when Prodrive's test driver, Tom Hunt, tried out revised tyres on a concrete corner of Bruntingthorpe Airfield in Britain. They were wholly unsuitable conditions for motorcycle-width snow tyres, but an excellent means of establishing that stud retention was vastly improved. The test paid off handsomely in much colder conditions the following winter.

At the end of February, McRae completed a remarkable Subaru hat-trick with a rousing triumph on the Safari. It was touch and go towards the end, as the alternator went sick during a long section across the plains south-west of Nairobi, and as the current dwindled, he resorted to switching off one of the fans and a fuel pump. The water temperature soared, the team prayed and, at the last gasp, the engine survived. It was ample revenge for the 1996 defeat and proof to McRae's critics that he could drive with guile and restraint.

Outsiders are generally outside bets in Corsica. Colin McRae's 1997 victory was clinched at the last gasp in the teeth of fierce local opposition.

The team had had to resort to its share of guile and restraint too. During the recce, one of its Trooper support vehicles had become stranded in the bush south of Nairobi in a particularly violent storm. A Masai tribesman was hired to guard it and the mechanics promised to return when the weather improved. A number of rescue attempts were defeated by the conditions and, sensing that this might become a full-time job, the guard built a palisade round the marooned Isuzu. In the end, a four-wheel-drive Bedford lorry was hired. Just when it seemed that the Trooper would be yanked from the morass, the driver stalled the engine. It emerged that the starter motor was broken. The mechanics sensed another wasted trip – all the more so when the driver crawled beneath and tied a rope round the front propshaft; the Bedford was a diesel. To their astonishment, the lawnmower technique worked like a charm. Ingenuity and persistence were rewarded.

There were some fine victories elsewhere too, notably another outstanding performance from McRae in Corsica. It wasn't a rally he knew particularly well and it has long been an event that foreigners find hard to win. If it hadn't rained in places, the outcome could easily have been very different. Any of four drivers might have won at the commencement of the final, 21-mile stage between Propriano and Ajaccio, but as it began to drizzle once more, the odds tilted a fraction in McRae's favour. In places, he had to nurse his soft Pirellis to avoid destroying them on the abrasive, coarse-grained 'red asphalt' that used to be such a feature of the island, but the rain did for the raucous two-wheel-drive 306s of François Delecour and Gilles Panizzi, and try as he might, Sainz was unable to prevent McRae regaining 15 seconds to snatch victory by eight.

The team celebrated with gusto that night, but it was already becoming clear that there were chinks in the armour. The Pirellis had been nothing like as effective on asphalt in Catalonia only days previously, and both cars had retired in Portugal with blown engines.

No worries for Colin McRae: the swashbuckling Scot soon made up the ground lost in the fog, pulverising the opposition to win the first RAC fought out almost entirely in the forests of Wales.

The wins mounted up, but so did the engine failures. In New Zealand, McRae was a minute ahead after just seven stages and in the process of routing the opposition when the flat-four blew. It was some consolation that Eriksson held off Sainz to secure his second victory of the year, thanks in part to a bizarre incident when the Spaniard collided with a sheep. Unlike sheep, unfenced roads are practically unheard of in New Zealand. At least Sainz retrieved second. To McRae, who had passed the wreckage of Mäkinen's Lancer minutes before retiring himself, it was the greatest disappointment of the season.

The engine failures stemmed from the WR Car redesign and had been narrowed down to the camshaft drive. Replacing plastic cam pulleys with aluminium made no worthwhile difference. FHI took a hand, establishing that different harmonics affecting the belt were at the root of the problem. It's an area of considerable stress on the flat-four, partly because it uses a single toothed belt – the longest on any production car at the time – to drive all four cams. The solution was to redesign the belt tooth profile and the tensioner, while increasing the belt wrap on the crankshaft pulley. It was an awkward job, as it would have been all too easy to increase friction.

Unfortunately, there had been five engine-related retirements by the time a cure was found and a few other setbacks too; McRae was leading until he nudged a bank and broke the steering on the Acropolis; Eriksson was well placed when terrifyingly, the steering seized mid-corner and he rolled; he finished third in Indonesia, when McRae charged into a commanding lead, just as he had in 1996, only to crash when the afternoon rains came. He managed to drag the wreckage as far as service in Pematang Siantar, but this time the engine had suffered too much.

As the year progressed, the pitfalls in the WR Car rules became apparent too. Lapworth and his right-hand man, Loriaux, were insistent that wide-track suspension was best: it gave more grip and more wheel travel, and it reduced load transfer. However,

the drivers – McRae in particular – grumbled that it was leading to understeer. Under pressure, the engineers agreed to give McRae a narrow-track car for New Zealand, essentially refitting Group A equipment. The job was nothing like as straightforward as it sounds. A fiddly, painstaking business, it was eventually completed late at night in the workshop in Auckland. It involved not just changing the suspension links, but the driveshafts, and a good deal of careful adjustment of the geometry. While Eriksson won with the wide-track type, there was no denying McRae's electrifying pace when he was running. The narrow-track option therefore survived and indeed, remained a source of frequent, if low-level friction between engineers and drivers until 2000.

The end of the season echoed the glories of 1995. McRae galloped to three straight victories, outpointing Liatti at Sanremo, when there was more than a suggestion of team orders, then holding off Mäkinen in a knife-edge finish in Australia, giving the team eight wins in all (its biggest World Championship haul in a season) and the manufacturers' crown for the third year in succession. The home crowd had another RAC win to celebrate – McRae's third in as many attempts. That would have been a remarkable achievement in any circumstances, given the treacherous nature of British forests in November, but all the more so as he dropped a chunk of time at dawn on the first forest stage, when he was slowed by fog. The tables were turned with extraordinary swiftness once visibility improved; Grist reckoned he had never been driven so quickly through a forest in his life.

But there had been too many accidents and too many engine failures to deprive Mäkinen of the title. McRae had become disenchanted. If his Subaru contract hadn't been watertight, he would have joined Ford for 1998.

By the end of the following season, an eight-year partnership had come to a close and McRae had gladly agreed to abandon a winning car in preference for a Focus that had scarcely been tested. It was a sour end to a relationship that had produced so much and inspired so many.

Compared to previous years, it hadn't been much of a season. By June, McRae had scored three victories, among them his first on the Rally of Portugal. Even by his standards, it was a giddily dramatic success. He led for most of the distance, but as the finish neared, the odds tilted in favour Sainz and Toyota; in a bygone era, running first on the road would have been an unqualified blessing, because McRae would have had a dust-free run. However, two-minute intervals between the top cars had all but removed the hazards posed by dust and, instead, McRae became the latest driver to find that in dry conditions the first car loses time from sweeping loose gravel clear for its pursuers.

Sainz inched ever closer. With one 6.86-mile stage remaining, McRae's lead had shrunk to 6.8 seconds and there was plenty of gravel on the final test. Grimly, he acknowledged that he was likely to lose.

It is difficult to imagine many other drivers winning under the circumstances. McRae had dropped four seconds on Toyota's unofficial mid-stage timing, but somehow he wriggled free. Sainz fell short by 2.1 seconds – the narrowest margin ever on a European round of the World Championship. He could reflect only that the closing miles had been so sandy that they had been 'like a beach'. At the critical moment the road hadn't 'cleaned' after all.

McRae was elated and intrigued to learn that it had been the closest-ever winning margin, but he confessed that he hadn't relished being hunted down.

'When you're in front, you've got it there and all you can do is lose it. When you're behind, it's a different feeling. It looked safe, but then I relaxed a bit too much earlier and let them take a bit too much. It was getting a wee bit close for comfort at the end. But really, at the end of the day, the win is the thing. It doesn't matter how much you win or lose by,' he said.

Rain played its part in allowing him to emulate Alén and become the second non-Frenchman to win Corsica twice in a row.

Pirelli's RE intermediate was superb, although it's worth noting that the Scot was also quickest on the longest stage of the rally, Morosaglia-Campile, which was almost completely dry. When a fuse popped out of Auriol's Corolla on the Acropolis, he pounced once more to claim his second Greek victory. Pirelli's faithful XR3 (a new name, but with the same tread pattern as the 1970s SG35) had excelled itself again on Europe's most punishing rally and McRae had defied the odds by staying in contention, despite running near the front for most of the distance. Reliability had played its part too. He had been the one driver not to hit trouble in the final leg, yet victory had been snatched against the run of play.

'I think it was a bonus. If we were going to beat Didier, it would have been by the very smallest of margins I'm sure, but it was going to be a struggle with three stages to go,' Grist admitted afterwards.

Mäkinen and Mitsubishi were struggling to sort out the Lancer Evo V, and the team

Back in Cheltenham, Colin McRae and Nicky Grist celebrated an emphatic RAC success and Subaru's third consecutive World Championship.

was privately questioning the Finn's commitment. For Subaru, the titles beckoned. As McRae pointed out, he wasn't faced with trying to make up ground for once – but he added that most rallies were much too closely fought to make his points lead anything like comfortable. It turned out to be his last World Championship win for the team.

The Impreza WRC98, which had been introduced for the Monte, looked to be a judicious improvement. The manifolds had been reshaped, a bigger turbo had released a little more power and careful attention to the anti-lag system maintained response. The crankshaft, con rods and flywheel were all new, all a fraction lighter than before. As the restrictor blocked the obvious route to increasing power, minimising friction and inertia assumed greater importance. STi took a hand in engine development once more.

Prodrive made progress in other areas too. Liatti had experimented with electronically controlled dampers on the previous year's RAC, and in New Zealand in 1998, Lapworth's prophecy that a Subaru rally car would use three active differentials was at last fulfilled. Consideration had been given to using a Swedish-made Haldex rear differential. However, a hydraulic wet-clutch type was preferred, with its own pump producing 50bar pressure. The gain was nothing like as great as it had been from introducing active control of the front and centre differentials – McRae veered between the active and passive types in New Zealand, in fact – but it offered greater scope for adjustment.

That scope was deliberately reserved chiefly for the engineers. An extra knob on the dashboard did allow the drivers to alter a single parameter of their choice affecting rear differential behaviour, but no more. The potential for exploring a blind alley rather than a fresh dimension was too great.

McRae's inspirational quality was exemplified by the Rally of Argentina when, for once, it looked as though Mäkinen might be overthrown. To the Finn's dismay, his arch-rival succeeded in beating him on

Colin McRae's commitment was unfailingly a sight to behold, but despite three wins, his 1998 World Championship campaign faded markedly.

Chamico-Ambul, a long, winding stage north of Mina Clavero, on which he had traditionally put the opposition to the sword. Mäkinen shattered his own stage record by half a minute, only for McRae to undercut it by two seconds.

The duel continued on the rally's highest, roughest and most famous stages, El Condor and Giulio Cesare, 2,000 metres up in the foothills of the Andes. Between these protagonists there was more than a suspicion that it was going to be settled by a knock-out. Just when it seemed that he had Mäkinen against the ropes, McRae burst over a crest to find a boulder in the middle of the road. He couldn't avoid it altogether and hobbled out of the stage with a rear wheel wedged in its arch. It would have been impossible to free it at all unaided if the tyre hadn't obligingly burst.

Once it had, McRae dismantled what was left of the rear suspension, smashed the lateral link straight with a rock, refitted it and hurtled into the time control two seconds within his maximum lateness. To general disbelief, he was then fastest on the descent of El Condor, minus the rear anti-roll bar. Thanks largely to the road penalties, he had lost too much time to improve on fifth. It was a meagre reward for an extraordinary performance.

It contrasted somewhat with the Sanremo Rally, when he left the pre-event shake-down early and thus spent much of the weekend trying to adjust the handling to his liking. He finished third, well behind Liatti and, more to the point, even further behind Mäkinen.

Yet, in a sense, the season turned on another disappointment, when McRae finished a close fourth in Australia. Even some of the best drivers had yet to appreciate at that point that running at the front on dry, loose-surface rallies had become a crippling handicap when routes were short and competition was tight. Mäkinen had supposed that victory would be as good as certain once he'd completed the straightforward task of picking off Sainz's leading Toyota in the final leg. He was aghast

to discover that McRae, running sixth on the road and a minute behind, was reeling him in hand over fist.

Earlier suspension and driveshaft problems no longer mattered. With two stages to go, McRae scythed into the lead and the World Championship reckoning. Then, with only five competitive miles remaining, the turbo blew. Mäkinen retrieved his victory and became odds-on favourite for the world title, while McRae was out of the running. It was Subaru's first turbo failure on a rally in five years.

The team had become almost exclusively reliant on McRae. Eriksson had been discarded after the Swedish, Liatti had unaccountably gone into decline on dirt rallies, which were very much in the majority, and experimentation with other drivers, such as Jarmo Kytölehto and Colin's brother Alister (who was drafted in for the Rally of Great Britain) failed to produce results.

The Rally GB – as the RAC had become – typified the malaise: Colin was leading, locked in combat with Burns's Mitsubishi, until his engine fell sick and expired smokily at the service area in Builth Wells; Alister crashed in the fog and Vatanen, who had been recalled to try a new type of gearbox, dropped out with engine trouble. It was very definitely time for a change.

The new season brought a new car, a new driver line-up and a new sense of purpose, yet there was no disguising that Subaru had been weakened by McRae's departure. Indeed, the team was at its most vulnerable since it had first embarked on a full World Championship assault in 1994.

The driver line-up was spearheaded by Burns and Kankkunen. It was a potentially effective combination, but although he had scored two major wins at Mitsubishi, Burns had yet to contest certain rallies and his lack of experience made him a long-odds bet as a title contender. Kankkunen, who had first won a World Championship rally in 1985 and had since become champion four times, certainly didn't want for experience. Unflappable and abundantly talented, he was an immense asset but, at 39, he no longer

shared quite the cavalier scorn for self-preservation that marked out McRae and Mäkinen.

Initially, Prodrive also planned to run one of Kankkunen's former Ford teammates, Bruno Thiry. A highly capable driver with a strong record in semi-works Subarus, amongst other cars, the genial Belgian unaccountably failed to thrive in the works team. His best result was fifth on the Monte, and after crashing on the Tour of Corsica he was paid to sit at home.

The official line that the manufacturers' title was the goal tacitly recognised that none of the drivers was likely to become World Champion. There were doubts over the car, too. As it often did, Subaru began the season with the previous year's version, on the basis that extra development time was worthwhile and that the Monte's uncertain weather ensured that drivers and tyres tended to make the difference, rather than the machinery.

Kankkunen put in an exemplary drive to finish second, but for most of the rally, the top Subaru driver was Panizzi, driving a private Impreza. There were accusations of illegal practising, as there often were against him at the time. They were not proven and, more to the point, he was a double French

Champion running on Michelins, as opposed to the works cars' Pirellis. It was an eye-catching performance, for Panizzi's four-wheel-drive experience was minimal.

Burns – never a Monte fan – was an out-of-sorts eighth. It was a jolt to the system. Like many drivers, he had struggled initially to adapt to Mitsubishi's unique, part-time four-wheel-drive arrangement, in which a sprag clutch connected drive to the front wheels solely when the rears began to spin. Settling into the more conventional Impreza ought to have been like returning to a much-loved old home. Instead, he found that the engine felt lethargic and the handling wasn't as precise as he would have wished. The old faithful H-pattern gearbox inherited from the Legacy had come to seem primitive, too; Subaru had been the only manufacturer with a non-sequential gearbox for the two preceding seasons.

Many of those doubts were answered with the launch of the WRC99 on the Swedish. It used the new gearbox that Vatanen had tried the previous November on the Rally GB and, under the direction of Terry Stamper, the team had found a little more power. There was a clear link between engine and transmission, in the form of uprated electronics.

New drivers brought a new zest to Subaru's 1999 campaign. After a difficult start, Richard Burns emerged as the team's pacesetter.

The gearbox was much the biggest undertaking. It was similar to the original in many respects, in that it was a six-speed, non-synchromesh design and some of the internals were the same, but as the quest for extra performance intensified, it was recognised that a manual H-pattern change would no longer suffice. Prodrive had no intention of catching up with the opposition. The new gearbox was intended to be a step ahead, combining the ease of use and the rapid gearchange of the semi-automatic sequential type pioneered on the Corolla with the flexibility of an H-pattern. Gearchanges were made by pushing or pulling a lever (known as a paddle at Prodrive) on the steering column, but buttons on the dashboard allowed the driver to find first or reverse instantly in the event of a spin, rather than fishing through each ratio in turn before restarting, which was unavoidable on a sequential unit.

It was an admirable objective, but some of those involved with the project wonder if it was worth the heartache. The 'reset' provision meant that the internals couldn't be laid out as in a purely sequential gearbox, and this made designing the hydraulics and electronics that controlled the gearchange vastly more complicated, because the mechanism had to move in two planes. Loriaux has no hesitation in describing Rick Townend, Prodrive's electronics expert, as 'a genius'. It also led to an increase in hydraulic pressure. While the differentials continued to run at 50bar (as they did into the 21st century) the gearchange required its own system running at 70bar, with a failsafe mode of 140bar. There were (and are) three hydraulic systems altogether, with a separate circuit for the steering. Nonetheless, designing and programming them turned out to be only half the challenge.

It is human nature that drivers will be quick to announce that they lost more time because the car wouldn't restart or wouldn't engage reverse; they tend not to return to service wreathed in smiles, telling the world that they dropped only ten seconds with a spin thanks to the ingenious reset button on the dashboard. That said, it is difficult to recall a rally won through the ability to re-engage first in a hurry.

One of the aims was that gearbox and engine worked in unison. Semi-automatic operation not only increased the speed at which gears could be changed, but made it all but impossible to miss a gear, with a consequent benefit in time saved and gear damage reduced.

Revised electronics, produced jointly by FHI, GEMS and Prodrive, included an electronic fly-by-wire accelerator for the first time. The electronics provided the link between the engine and the gearchange, and they also made it possible to specify a larger turbo once more, obtaining extra power and torque. More advanced programming countered throttle lag and made it possible to match accelerator travel to driver preference. Prodrive also took the opportunity to experiment with traction and yaw control. The new arrangement also demanded a more powerful data logger with a colour display. Its memory had grown to 4MB; a vast increase over the original. It was filled soon enough.

'It had a couple of pages that you could display and it was superb: one page for the drivers and ten for the engineers, because once you start to get an automatic gearbox in it, you needed to look at so many different parameters,' Moore explained. 'Fine when they're all working, but if you have a small glitch with it, you can't go, "Oh, I know what that is". You have to look at the data. If you've got it all on one page, you can go, "It's that sensor," and change it, even without actually interrogating the logger. It's actually a very useful diagnostic tool. It doesn't have to be an engineer that does it.'

Mechanics used to spanners and screwdrivers were introduced to the world of computer analysis.

The new car didn't cover itself in glory on its first appearance, the three WRC99s finishing fifth, sixth and tenth. It was a satisfying week for Burns, who got the better of a prolonged duel with Kankkunen and the conclusion was that Pirelli's snow tyres

hadn't been quite on a par with Michelin's.

However, there were soon some uncomfortable questions being asked about the WRC99. For the second year running, there were no works Imprezas at the end of the Safari and it triggered a lengthy, nerve-racking inquest at Banbury. Burns's retirement was frustrating, but straightforward enough. He was neck and neck with McRae and Mäkinen, in with a good chance of repeating his 1998 victory, when a bolt sheared and the suspension collapsed as he headed down Eldama Ravine, not far from the Ugandan border.

The concern surrounded Kankkunen and Thiry, who were both halted by defective electronics. Worse still, there was no obvious explanation. Kankkunen's car fired up sweetly enough with a new battery. The data logger confirmed that the ECU had switched off, but couldn't say how. When Juha's brother Timo, his gravel-note driver, attacked the section again, the car ran perfectly. Prodrive resorted to numbering trusted ECUs and recording their mileages until a shake-and-bake test rig

back at Banbury eventually uncovered the fault. The improved ECUs were flown out to the next rally as hand luggage. It was a reminder that while electronics offer dazzling possibilities, there is nothing more insidious than an invisible failure.

Burns was livid after Portugal, not with the team, but the press. He had finished fourth and rounded on *Motoring News* journalists, whom he felt hadn't given him due credit for a heart-in-mouth effort in a car that failed to inspire much confidence. While Kankkunen settled contentedly into the wide-track car, Burns was more at ease in the narrow-track version. Both maintained that the handling left something to be desired nevertheless, and it was agreed that the tyres needed redesigning. The narrower KM was quicker than the K, but wasn't used as much as the drivers might have liked, because the tread was too unstable. The solution was to redesign the tread with a slight curve on the blocks, maintaining feel while enhancing grip.

'Because of the way I drive, I've got to have precision and very good feel at the front

The apprentices during their first stint at Subaru, Richard Burns and Robert Reid had grown into one of the most formidable combinations in the sport on their return in 1999. Their attention to detail was unsurpassed.

of the car, and if I'm into a corner I like to be able to adjust the angle of the car without it giving loads of oversteer, just to be able to have this direct front,' Burns explained. 'They worked a lot on the geometry and I couldn't get it with the wide-track car. I couldn't achieve that feeling, so I'd much rather know that I wouldn't have ultimate performance, but go with better feel. Juha could drive around it.'

Kankkunen felt that modifications to the suspension and differentials were just as important as new tyres. He missed the Tour of Corsica in favour of a lengthy test in Greece, in which significant alterations were made to the rear geometry, and alternative differential programmes were tried.

'We got the car more to the balance, not so much oversteering, so it was little bit even understeering side, but that gave you possibility to drive a little bit more aggressive and still it was holding not that much sideways, but much more corner speed. You had to drive it aggressive that it didn't understeer.

'Richard's driving style was very similar to mine, so that you could throw the car into the corner, not to get it so that you had to look on the side windows only! You could get it going forwards as well. Richard was used to drive with Mitsubishi, which was very, very narrow track and I liked the wide track. It was struggling a little bit on the narrow road, but when you got to the faster speed and to the faster road it was really good. So you have to sort of find a compromise,' Kankkunen said.

It was a question of fine-tuning. Despite spending the previous year in the only other WR car with a longitudinal engine, the Escort, the Finn had been impressed with the Impreza's superior weight distribution and its long-travel suspension from the outset.

In the meantime, the Tarmac rallies had done nothing to dispel the view that Prodrive had become a team with its back to the wall. On dry asphalt, Pirelli's tyres were no longer competitive (the Imprezas were harried by Armin Schwarz's works Skoda for a time in Catalonia) and as the team neared 12 months

without a win, rumours spread that Japan had delivered an ultimatum: either Prodrive won a rally by the Acropolis in June or the programme would be wound up. Prodrive sources have always hotly denied that there was even a shred of truth in the story, pointing out that Subaru's devotion to four-wheel drive made the World Rally Championship the ideal form of motorsport.

Even if the cars weren't winning, there was a feeling at Banbury that progress was being made. The new recruits were ready to try new developments, and in Argentina any doubts over the competitiveness of the car or the drivers were banished. Auriol was the best of the rest, half a minute behind in his works Corolla. The Imprezas led for 15 of the 22 stages, and at the last gasp Kankkunen claimed his first victory at World Championship level since Portugal in 1994. It was a conclusive, but controversial success, for Burns had led most of the way and as Auriol fell back, the plan had been that the Subaru men would ease off and maintain their positions.

Even Kankkunen had expected his younger teammate to be the victor but, running second, he enjoyed marginally better road conditions and the two certainly hadn't slowed enough for this factor to be discounted. Robbie Head, Burns's gravel note driver, was dispatched to the final stage with a board to display 'pit signals' to each driver. Kankkunen insisted that he had misunderstood the signal and completed the stage 2.4 seconds in front. Burns didn't find out until he returned to service. To say that he felt cheated would be a gross understatement – and following McLaren's clumsy imposition of team orders in the Australian Grand Prix a few months before, he knew that ordering the Finn to take road penalties and fall into line would almost certainly have triggered a severe FIA sanction.

Some drivers argue that their teammates are their most dangerous opponents, because they have the same type of car; lose to your teammate and you're struggling for an excuse. Teams sometimes argue that a little tension between the drivers is constructive and there are grounds for thinking that that was true in this case. They undoubtedly spurred each other on. In Greece, Burns rocketed ahead, then voluntarily surrendered the lead and dropped to fourth at the end of the first leg by taking 40 seconds of road penalties. The theory was that he would lose far more time by running first and acting as gravel plough on bone-dry dirt tracks, but there was no question that it added to the pressure on him, too: defeat by fewer than 40 seconds would have been humiliating.

He made up the lost time in two stages, but Mäkinen and Sainz were still hot on his heels, partly because the Impreza died twice in river crossings when the gearbox electronics went sick. Mäkinen slipped in front briefly and, although Burns was ahead, the rally was still very much open as the final leg headed into the mountains north of Agii Theodori. He was fighting alone after Kankkunen retired with collapsed rear suspension.

The first two stages were brutally rough and, at Burns's suggestion, one of the gravel note crews, Timo Kankkunen and Ken Rees, went out at sunrise, *after* the other gravel note crews had been through, and rolled some of the most menacing boulders out of the way. Whether it made a significant difference is difficult to say, but it undoubtedly gave Burns a cleaner line than his pursuers were expecting. It provided a little boost to his confidence.

Burns drove beautifully, keeping something in hand through the roughest opening miles, then going on to the attack. After the first loop, both Sainz and Mäkinen were nursing suspension damage and his victory was as good as assured. It was a testament to his ability and judgement, but also to the car. Later, he suggested that the difference between the Impreza and its rivals was that it was designed to bend, not break.

Once the team had gathered momentum, it became difficult to stop. Mäkinen had put the World Championship beyond the Subaru drivers' reach, but on dirt they had become the pacesetters. Burns and Loriaux finally

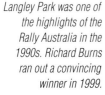

Langley Park was one of the highlights of the Rally Australia in the 1990s. Richard Burns ran out a convincing winner in 1999.

agreed on a compromise, in the form of medium-track suspension, which was first made available in Finland. A Finnish defeat is a rare thing on home ground, but Kankkunen was pushed to the limit to hold off his teammate, winning by just nine seconds. Burns was a close second once more in China, losing to Auriol thanks in large part to an incorrect tyre choice when it rained during the last leg. He rounded off the season with convincing victories in Australia and Britain, Kankkunen taking second in Wales. Sainz had offered stern resistance in Australia before being overpowered in the closing stages, but in Britain the Imprezas were in a class apart. Between them they led for all but the first stage. Burns was second in the drivers' championship and Subaru was second in the manufacturers' series, only four points behind Toyota. The rebuilding exercise had been carried out with awesome speed.

In any other year, the manufacturers' crown would have gone to Subaru, but in 1999, extra points were awarded to the three fastest cars on any stage televised live. It was roundly criticised as a gimmick that had no place in a sport that places some of its emphasis on endurance, and it was scrapped soon enough. However, it turned out that Auriol performed best for the cameras and the extra points tilted the contest in Toyota's favour.

The 2000 season didn't continue quite where 1999 had left off. Kankkunen was runner-up once more on the Monte, while Burns, who had been a close second after the first leg, retired when he was unable to restart from the overnight halt in Gap. The Impreza didn't take kindly to a temperature of −10° Celsius and it wasn't much consolation that a similar fault wiped out the Peugeots as well. The drivers finished in the same positions as they had on the previous year's Swedish, then completed the WRC99's career in the best possible manner, with first and second places on the Safari.

Pirelli played a prominent role in this triumph, for the Michelin teams were thrown on to the defensive almost at once. The Safari was not only the longest and roughest, but much the quickest event in the World

Championship. Averages sometimes approached 100mph and, at sustained speeds of that kind, run-flat tyres were pressed beyond their limits. Pirelli had concluded that EMI was not best suited to the terrain and concentrated on making tyres that were unlikely to puncture in the first place. Burns didn't have a single puncture, in fact, but Michelin felt that its EMI equivalent, ATS, would go the distance. A rash of flat tyres in the early sections proved otherwise and, once ahead, the Subarus were never seriously troubled.

But winning the Safari has never been a formality. Burns's engine began to overheat badly as he returned south towards Elementeita Drift, near Nakuru. The car lasted the section, then stopped and refused to restart at the next time control. Service was forbidden at that point and the engineers had to devise a solution and relay it to the crew over the radio. They were convinced that the engine would run if only the electronics would co-operate. After a few minutes, they suggested that he poured cold water over the appropriate sensor. Sure enough, the engine restarted.

In the second half of 1999, Richard Burns was the driver to beat, his increasing confidence complemented by growing experience.

4 In search of the last five per cent

No one who attended the first overseas test of the Impreza WRC2000 is likely to forget it. In late winter, the test team took the new car to Catalonia for a back-to-back comparison with the WRC99 near Girona. It was an unpromising start. Burns was unwell and consequently not in a good mood when he turned up, instantly declaring that it wasn't a good choice of road. Scolding finished, he fired the old car down the dirt track to record a benchmark time, then clambered aboard the new one.

'When we test, I always take times, every time, and our judgement's not always based on that, but it's something. You get into the routine, you get to the end of the test run, Richard'll say a few things and then he'll glance across and see what the time was. It's all involved in the process of making your mind up,' Robert Reid explained.

'We got to the end of the run, he looked across, looked down at the time and he said something he very, very seldom says to me: "Are you sure?"

'And I said, "Yep".

'"Oh. We'd better do another run then, hadn't we?" Did another run, and again, similar result, because it was that classic ingredient you always look for: it doesn't feel that quick, but on the watch, it is. It was easy and to a large extent it solved a lot of the issues that Richard had had with the '99 car in various widths. It just did everything he wanted it to do.'

'I was like, "When do we start?" On the stages, it just translated as well. That was a brilliant car, a massive change,' Burns recalled.

The new car – generally known by its prototype name, as the P2000 – was instantly a second per mile faster than its predecessor, running on guessed suspension settings. On that basis, it would be more than three minutes quicker in the course of a World Championship rally. It promised to make every other car obsolete overnight. It wasn't a lengthy test: Burns left soon enough, content that the objective had been met.

Even so, there was a sense of trepidation as well as anticipation when the team headed for the new machine's first rally in Portugal, in March 2000, as there always is until any promising car proves to have the reliability to match its speed. To add to the air of intrigue, strenuous efforts to keep the press and public at arm's length continued as late as the shakedown, the final pre-rally test.

The rally more than justified the belief that Subaru had something worth hiding, for Burns was unstoppable. Ultimately, he finished only six seconds ahead of Marcus Grönholm's 206, but there had been an inevitability about his success almost since the start, and had the car been trouble free the rally would have been over as a contest by the halfway mark.

It was far from trouble free. Burns took the lead on the fourth stage, then lost it when the power steering failed. It's a serious setback on any modern rally car, as it forces the driver to fight not just the hydraulic rams without assistance, but a limited slip differential in the front axle as well. To the team's consternation, it turned out that the replacement steering pump had been wrongly assembled. Burns had dropped 40 seconds before the P2000 was

The P2000 was an overnight sensation. It remains Richard Burns's favourite rally car and at times, they were in a league apart.

genuinely back on song. It was a temporary respite: he came close to retirement while cruising down the motorway to the rest halt in Oporto that night when he was run off the road – unintentionally – by a Toyota service vehicle. The collision left the Impreza looking somewhat the worse for wear, but fundamentally unscathed.

Then it was noticed that his car was leaking petrol in *parc ferme*. The fuel tank was pressurised and had therefore cracked its cover. When he arrived at service, the tank was bulging so much that it was on the point of falling out. In tests, the mechanics had always refuelled from jerry cans. During the rally, the official refuelling crew used an electric pump and it emerged that the pipe connecting the auxiliary and main tanks wasn't big enough to cope with the increased flow. Modifications were hastily planned.

Burns overhauled Grönholm towards the end of the second leg, only to lose more time and the lead once again when driving in his opponent's dust at nightfall. He didn't conceal his anger and yet it was difficult to believe that it was anything but another temporary setback.

Grönholm's resistance was valiant and in vain. Like the WRC97, the P2000 won at the first attempt. A near-run thing, it was nevertheless a triumphant demonstration of the team's capabilities. It was an emotional success too. Loriaux, the car's designer – the apprentice engineer when Burns was an

apprentice driver and they had won the British Championship seven years previously – was in tears at the final service in Ponte de Lima. Back in Banbury, at a champagne reception to commemorate the feat, he joked that it proved that if a monkey is seated at a piano, he can be taught to play.

A born enthusiast who had conceived the ambition to work for Prodrive as a teenaged spectator when it was running BMWs in Belgium, Loriaux's genial, relaxed manner is deceptive. At work, his attention to detail borders on the obsessive. Outwardly, the new Impreza was hard to distinguish from its predecessor. Under the skin, around 80% of the car was new.

Prodrive reasoned that the heightened competitiveness of the World Championship demanded a new car every three years or so. It also recognised that the nature of the sport and tightly written regulations didn't give much scope for revolutionary change; despite far fewer restrictions on electronics and active systems than in Formula 1, the environment made it difficult if not impossible to exploit those freedoms despite technological advances.

There was an additional incentive for concentrating on the performance aspect. A new Impreza road car, codenamed the 44S, was in the wings, and the business of changing bodyshells would be complicated enough without a simultaneous mechanical overhaul. The transfer was therefore planned in two stages, with the great majority of the new running gear built and developed before the new bodyshell.

'There's nothing dramatic, just the percentages game, but that's the whole point. If we've made nearly every component on the car five per cent better, a five per cent improvement is a big step. That's the mentality these days. We are on the flatter part of the [development] curve with these WR Cars. On the other hand, the positive side of that is if we can go further up the curve, then it's harder work for everybody else to follow us. I think that approach is going to pay off. The car is just a little bit better everywhere,' Lapworth commented.

Describing each new Impreza as an evolution, not a revolution is practically a refrain. The P2000 was certainly an evolution, a painstaking, incremental reassessment of almost every aspect of the car, but in this instance, that process amounted to a revolution.

As Lapworth assumed greater responsibility for running the team, Loriaux was in overall charge of the design for the first time. His overriding aim was to find more grip and traction by improving weight distribution. It was already one of the Impreza's strong points, thanks to the lightweight flat-four, but Loriaux found ample scope for refinement. There were the usual changes – marginally lighter engine internals, a stiffer rollcage, better aerodynamics – but although it notionally shared the WRC99's bodyshell, engine and gearbox, the P2000 amounted to a new car.

Lapworth stressed the importance of ancilliary components: 'I think a dressed engine is about 170 kilos and a bodyshell weighs – these aren't actual figures – 300 kilos, let's say 75 kilos for a gearbox and 25 kilos for a diff. What's that, about 600 kilos? There's another 600 kilos of odds and ends that you can move around and that makes a big difference. I'm talking about everything – about co-driver's equipment and map lights to fire extinguishers and tool kits – that it is possible to move.'

Every conceivable component was lowered and, where possible, brought within the wheelbase. The engine and gearbox were repositioned, the petrol tank was moved from the boot to its standard position beneath the rear seat pan. That in itself was an awkward task, because it had to allow for the propshaft and it was difficult to achieve the necessary capacity. It therefore took the form of a 'saddle bag' tank with interconnecting pipes, as well as a pipe to a much smaller auxiliary tank in the boot. The pedals were bottom-hinged for the first time,

Revisions for 2000 included repositioning the co-driver and redesigning some of his equipment.

like a racing car's, while the alternator was repositioned low down at the front of the engine, driven off a six-inch shaft.

The bodyshell itself had a new propshaft tunnel and much of the switchgear was moved to a panel on top of the tunnel between the seats, thereby shifting a little more mass rearwards and downwards.

One of Loriaux's personal triumphs was the vertical turbo. Japan had been most insistent that this was not to be contemplated, because it would be impossible to lubricate. However, Loriaux was convinced, not only that resiting it would usefully aid his quest for better weight distribution and improve the efficiency of the induction system, but that it could be lubricated.

It was an empirical process. Working with Clive Wilcox, a veteran ex-Andy Rouse mechanic, he sawed up a number of turbos to establish where the oil galleries ran. With the knowledge gained, the development team devised a new oil system that would function when it was tilted far beyond the recommended 20 degrees. Loriaux concedes that at first it dripped a little. But it worked.

'My motto is everything is possible if you try hard enough,' he observed.

The rear differential was new, releasing a little more suspension travel, and while MacPherson struts were retained all round, every part was redesigned, further extending suspension travel and saving weight. In the process, Loriaux solved the track conundrum. He had realised that it wasn't the narrow track that some drivers preferred, but the geometry that went with it. Careful attention to camber, castor and bumpsteer convinced all drivers that the wide track was best. A three-year debate ended in Portugal.

The crew themselves were part of the design process. When Loriaux informed Burns and Reid that he intended to lower the gearbox by 10–15mm, Reid suggested that perhaps he could sit lower in the car; a human being weighs about the same as a gearbox. A lowered seating position was therefore tried in the later months of 1999. In the 2000 car, the co-driver sat 50mm lower and 80mm further back than he had 12 months previously.

'So far as I was concerned, the further back and lower down I am, the better. It's as far away from the sharp end when it all goes wrong,' Reid said. 'Certainly then having sat in that position, you don't want to go back to sitting higher. I think co-drivers split into two – well, they split into lots of categories – but they can be split into two categories and that's those who only look out the window when they have to and those that only look at the notes when they have to. I would say I am definitely in the former category and therefore I found it quite easy. A lot of the reading of the notes and the timing and everything comes from the feeling in the car.'

Loriaux's quest for the ideal chassis extended to the co-driver's equipment. With two 16-bit processors plus a data logger on board as part of an enhanced electronics system, he didn't see why the navigator needed a separate time and distance recorder of his own. The Coralba – hardly a heavyweight item, in fact – was therefore discarded in favour of an extra screen for the co-driver, sited lower and more centrally. It was a far cry from Reid's first taste of a works Subaru, when he climbed into Alén's Rally of Portugal Legacy for a test, to find it

Floor-hinged pedals were yet another sign of Christian Loriaux's attention to detail. They also contributed to a lower centre of gravity.

was fitted with Ilkka Kivimäki's electronic Halda and a pair of analogue Heuer clocks.

It was a team exercise. Graham Neil was primarily responsible for the P2000's new cooling system and took a hand in the aerodynamics, Simon Carrier was in charge of much of the design work on screen, while Adrian Mitson, the test team manager, and Farley were also heavily involved. Stevens played a part in shaping both the interior and the exterior. Around a dozen people were responsible for reinventing the Impreza. Much of the redesign was computerised, but a significant proportion of the process involved mocking up parts by hand in the traditional way. Stem to stern computerisation is easier when a car is entirely new.

The focus on weight distribution took two forms. Loriaux aimed to lower the centre of gravity, but also to reduce the polar moment of inertia – to minimise the dumb-bell effect of having heavy items outside the wheelbase. Repositioning the fuel tank fulfilled both objectives. The lower centre of gravity enhanced roadholding, while the lower polar moment of inertia made the car more manoeuvrable. This wasn't necessarily an unmixed blessing. A more responsive car isn't always easier to drive and some previous competition cars designed to have low polar moments of inertia have been renowned for evil handling.

Lapworth was confident that a steel-bodied, three-box saloon built to withstand the rigours of Greek backroads wasn't in danger of straying into that territory.

'There's an area in the middle. There's a number called the dynamic index, which in layman's terms is the relationship between the polar moment of inertia and the wheelbase. It tells you a little bit about how the car will handle. It is possible to go too far, to the point where the car is nervous, but I think with a four-wheel-drive car, where by definition the engine is at the front and it's got a rear diff and so on, I don't think it's an issue with a car with a two-and-a-half-metre wheelbase and the sort of weight of components you've got in a rally car.

'I don't think we're likely to reach the point where the cars become undriveable. They may be a little bit more nervous in the really fast, bumpy stuff – there may be a trade-off – but I think overall, if you think the average speed of the World Championship is 100km/h, it's generally pretty bloody twisty. You're looking for a car that's good when it's twisty,' he said.

Within weeks of the P2000's launch, Burns was looking a short-odds favourite for the World Championship. If the gearchange hadn't gone sick for a time in the second leg, he would very probably have won a prolonged duel with McRae's Focus in Catalonia, but while second was a mild disappointment, it was by some margin Subaru's best result on dry asphalt since 1998. In Argentina, he stretched his points lead with an outstanding victory, leaving the opposition trailing disconsolately in often wet and foggy conditions. The 68-second winning margin didn't reflect the P2000's blistering turn of speed, for Burns was hampered by a succession of minor setbacks, ranging from a misfire, to periodic bouts of overheating, a broken handbrake bracket, worn pads and clutch trouble. None of it seemed to matter: there was performance in

New Zealand was one of the most bitter disappointments in 2000. Richard Burns was third and closing on Colin McRae when his engine blew up three stages from the finish, practically alongside Juha Kankkunen.

Richard Burns was in his element in Finland and in 2000, he was the only driver regularly capable of giving Marcus Grönholm a run for his money.

hand. He had been a shade lucky too, overshooting a junction and slithering into a boulder with a stage to run. It rolled harmlessly out of his way.

Kankkunen backed him up with fourth, despite skidding into a wall and getting stuck for a minute during the last leg.

'It was a lot more suited to my style,' Burns enthused. 'I could be precise, direct and it was spot-on. It reacted more – I wouldn't say violently, that's wrong – but it was just much, much more responsive. When you braked and turned, it did it, rather than, you know, sort of drifting it in somewhere. You drove it more precisely. I wouldn't say it was an easy car – it wasn't as easy as a '99 car, by quite a long way – but it just suited the way I wanted to drive.'

But as the months passed, the P2000's deficiencies became impossible to overlook. On the Acropolis, the new dampers caused major problems, the seals failing to cope with the heat and dust in the early stages. Kankkunen retrieved third in the end behind the works Fords, whereas Burns retired with

engine trouble. In New Zealand, Burns and Kankkunen were third and fifth when the flywheels shattered four stages from the end. They retired within yards of each other.

In Finland, the car was hardly to blame, but the initiative tilted further towards Grönholm and Peugeot. No rally places more emphasis on knowledge of the roads, which made Burns's performance in the first leg all the more impressive, as he was the one driver to keep Grönholm in sight. Second would have been no disgrace, but he overreached himself on the first stage the next morning and rolled heavily into the trees between the flying finish and the stop line. Kankkunen would have been a good deal higher than eighth if someone had remembered to install the wheel nut gun. He found out only when he stopped to change a puncture in mid-stage.

It rather summed up Kankkunen's season. For the first time in his career, one of the sport's supreme instinctive talents was confronted with a car he didn't much like.

'The car was probably one of the best, but still we were struggling quite a lot, all the

No rally driver can resist
a shorter line. A
workmanlike
performance from
Richard Burns netted
fourth place on the Tour
of Corsica.

time small, small things. It was supposed to
be Richard's winning year, so he was the first
driver basically on the team; so, of course,
the first driver gets the best – which is fair,
that is the way it goes, if you want to win
something. So the car was made mainly to
his mind and it didn't fit for me that well. It
was the same with Mitsubishi: everything
was made for Tommi and the rest of the boys
drove with what was left,' he recalled.

Cyprus ought to have suited the Impreza
down to the ground – indeed, it had been
won by Impreza drivers for the three
previous years, when it was part of the
European Championship. It was every bit as
rough and hot as the Acropolis, but much
more twisty. An average speed of 40mph on
a stage was good going and, mindful of the
Acropolis failings, Prodrive tested
thoroughly. Nevertheless, it was another
intensely frustrating rally, in which Burns
finished fourth and Kankkunen (after two
separate road penalties) was seventh.

A new damper problem emerged, the
hybrid Prodrive/Bilstein struts overheating

badly. As a temporary fix, the independent
reservoirs were repositioned under the
bonnet to take advantage of what little
cooling air there was. Burns also lost time
when the carbon fibre propshaft was
shattered by a flying stone, Loriaux was left
fielding enquiries that he would have done
better to trade a little speed for strength and
there were suggestions that preparation
standards had slipped.

Its creator conceded that the car wasn't as
reliable as he would have liked, but
countered that much of it was new, the old
car would not have been competitive if it had
been retained for much longer and he had
designed a car to reflect the changing nature
of the sport. Certainly it was more
complicated and more difficult to work on
than previous Imprezas, but there was no
longer any point in building a simple car that
could be fettled in five minutes. The
regulation intervals for service were 10, 20 or
45 minutes, never 5. More advanced
hydraulics and electronics were becoming
essential. The objective was not to avoid

them, but to make them tough enough for a hostile environment.

Reflecting on its growing sophistication, one of the mechanics described it as 'a touring car with a sumpguard'. Others could understand Loriaux's thinking, but commented that it made the mechanic's life harder: the power steering was a case in point, the pump being moved from the top to the recesses of the engine bay, next to the alternator.

The comfortable points lead had disappeared, along with the capacity to win at will. By the penultimate rally in Australia, Burns needed a victory or at least to beat Grönholm to stand any real chance of becoming World Champion in Britain; Peugeot's Tarmac mastery had all but guaranteed it the manufacturers' crown. It was a hotly fought and highly charged weekend, in which a tactical manoeuvre backfired nastily.

There was little to choose between Burns, Grönholm and Mäkinen as they began the last leg in Sotico, a new name for a familiar forest, Bunnings, which regularly settled the

outcome. Seeking to run as far back as possible and thereby to exploit the cleanest line on Western Australia's horribly slippery 'ball bearing' gravel, Burns stopped to change a 'puncture' in a time control. With a marshal's consent, it was entirely permissible, but a touch questionable, in that EMI-equipped tyres don't often go flat, especially when they haven't been used on a stage.

The Finns were furious, accusing Burns and Subaru of bad sportsmanship. After a distinctly patchy season, an angry but inspired Mäkinen scorched to a narrow victory.

'That was messy, very messy. It was a difficult call to know what to do there. It didn't really help us in the end. It probably fired Marcus up more than it would have if we hadn't done anything. Yeah, we shouldn't have done it and we shouldn't have been told to do it,' Burns reflected.

Grönholm was second, Burns third. Mäkinen's triumph didn't stand though, as post-event scrutiny revealed a non-standard Mitsubishi turbo and he was excluded. It was

A hat-trick on the Rally of Great Britain is a rare feat and Richard Burns's success provided a suitable climax to the P2000's works career.

almost as big a blow for Burns: Grönholm became the victor, by all of 2.7 seconds, and the gap between them grew by two extra points. The Rally GB would no longer be a winner-takes-all affair, for Grönholm could afford to finish behind him, sitting back and letting Burns slug it out with McRae.

In Wales, Burns could scarcely have made a worse start, crabbing out of the first forest stage, Saint Gwynno, with one of the rear wheels hanging on by a thread. He had teetered into a ditch, clouted a rock and smashed a hub. He was half a minute down instantly and in some danger of retiring within miles, as the service point was in Builth Wells and there was at least a chance that the police might deem the stricken Subaru to be unroadworthy. Luckily, there was plenty of time and Burns limped gently and punctually into the time control.

The mechanics' efforts were well rewarded. It took Burns only seven stages to climb from 21st to third and Grönholm was soon within his sights. Catching McRae was another matter entirely. Richard, at least, had nothing to lose, and on the second run at Rheola the pressure paid off. Quite why McRae was still pushing so hard when he had a commanding lead remains something of a mystery – he denied that he was seeking to put his fellow countryman in his place – but the ensuing roll inflicted mortal damage to the Focus. Grönholm was handed the lead on a plate, but had no intention of waging a risky, unnecessary duel with the Subaru man. Burns swept past on Margam and the last leg turned into a victory parade. He became the first driver since Timo Mäkinen in 1975 to win the rally three years running. Kankkunen backed him up with fifth place.

That was no mean feat, yet there was no denying the sense of making do with half a loaf.

'The most disappointing few weeks of my whole career were the last day of the RAC and the next couple of weeks, because to have damaged the car on the first stage, fixed it, gone on to win the rally and not win the championship was a very, very difficult thing to come to terms with,' Reid stated. 'You felt you'd done absolutely everything you could, yet somebody had done what they had to do better.

'It was frustrating, because that should have been Richard's championship year. I think at some point in every driver's career – and some of them never experience it at all – there is a car you really click with, and for Richard it was that car. I think that level of feeling of invincibility kind of lost us the championship, because to crash out to Marcus in Finland, trying to chase him and beat him, I think if we hadn't done that, we would have won the championship.'

Burns acknowledges that that was a serious error, but is just as regretful that he crashed at Sanremo when in second place and closing fractionally on the winner, Panizzi, on unofficial mid-stage timing. With Lapworth, it's the New Zealand flywheel failures that rankle. Someone observed that if the rallying season mirrored football, Burns would have been the 1999–2000 champion by a country mile. In 2000, driver and team failed to press home a winning advantage. By the end of the year, much of the P2000's performance advantage had gone, whereas the steady improvement in reliability came a little too late.

'Richard and myself, we felt a little bit that it was our own mistake. We had a good team, good drivers, everything was working, so we should have won the championship once in those two years, so it was also up to us a little bit that we didn't do as well as we should have been doing,' Kankkunen observed.

Losing, like winning, is a team effort.

The P2000's flaws cannot be overlooked, yet Burns's adjective, 'brilliant', is no overstatement. Few rally cars have raised performance so dramatically, fewer still within such a tight regulatory framework. Loriaux's fondest memory of his decade with Prodrive is that Portuguese win. Burns has had no hesitation in describing it as his favourite rally car. Its career as a works car ended after scarcely eight months in Cardiff that November, not because it was out of date, but because the new Impreza was starting to fill showrooms.

5 New shape, new beginnings

It has become an unchanging law of passenger car design that each model is bigger and heavier than the last. Customers want more refinement and more safety features. Fulfilling their wishes seems to involve making bulkier cars, and the Impreza has bowed to the trend.

To Prodrive, switching to the new model (sometimes known by its Subaru codename as the 44S, sometimes by its Prodrive codename as the S7) was a major exercise, but more to do with logistics and marketing – both important considerations – than performance. In compliance with Subaru's wishes, the WRC2001 was introduced for the 2001 Monte Carlo Rally.

The new road car's looks generated a neutral response at best – the Australian monthly, *Motor*, reflected widespread horror by nicknaming it 'Bugzilla' – but when Prodrive revealed the rally version in October 2000, Lapworth succeeded in striking an optimistic note.

'We've found some improvements yet again in terms of strength and stiffness, the aerodynamics are definitely better and it's another chance to further refine the packaging,' he reported. 'The weight distribution is a little bit better, the serviceability is a little bit better, so there are some good technical reasons for changing to the 44S.

'From past experience, having been through this process several times with rally cars and racing cars over the years, the car is an immediate improvement anyway when you carry over the settings that you used before, but then you find there are further refinements that help you to go even further. It may take a while before we get the best out of it, but you don't have to take a step backwards to go forwards.'

Loriaux, the man responsible for turning it into a rally car, maintained that there were advantages, notably bodyshell stiffness, but commented that the one merit in swapping from two doors to four was better access when a second spare wheel was fitted. Tactfully, he didn't add that the regulations rarely granted such a luxury.

Reverting to four doors also meant a drastic reshaping of the inner rear wheel arches. It would not have been allowed in Group A and might have constituted a potentially serious handicap. More liberal World Rally Car rules meant that there was no loss of suspension travel.

The new shape did provide undisputed aerodynamic benefits, though. Once more, Peter Stevens had been called in, partly to assess its aerodynamic properties and partly to liaise with STi on the look of the road car. He reported some unexpected gains. Work had begun in September 1999 and several hundred runs were made in the MIRA wind tunnel. Even at the final test, there were seven different rear wing profiles, six endplates and five deck profiles to try. Even so, the definitive wing was not seen in public until the 2001 Monte.

The rallying approach to aerodynamics is markedly different from racing. Stevens's emphasis was not on gaining massive downforce, because stiffer springs at higher speeds would compromise traction at low speeds and on slippery surfaces, but on

Echoing Formula 1, the steering wheel has become the home for an increasing array of functions on a rally car.

The familiar combination of a Bilstein strut and a trailing arm is dominated by a massive Alcon rear brake disc and caliper.

Richard Burns's sole victory in the Impreza WRC2001, in New Zealand, was the result of flawless teamwork. It was a major step on his way to the 2001 world title.

providing consistent downforce not just at both ends, but when the car was sliding. Stevens had been surprised to learn how much time a car spent sideways, even on asphalt. The rear wing was therefore designed to give maximum downforce at seven degrees of yaw, declining gently to the straightline value.

Rather than use the drag co-efficient, on the basis that it is 'useless' unless multiplied by the frontal area, Stevens preferred to measure forces and work on drag/brake horsepower figures.

'We have a philosophy on this, which is that for major improvements in the downforce, we are prepared to use about two horsepower, but normally we try not to have any horsepower penalty. In a Cd figure, it would seem fairly inefficient compared with the best, efficient road cars, but at 100mph, most road cars that you see would produce 200 or 300 pounds of lift and usually not

very well distributed between the front and rear.

'You see some rally cars and, plainly, once they're sliding it's a struggle to keep control of them, because there's lots of lift at the back and then it slides even more. It's self-defeating. We want the opposite. We want to play safe rather than play dangerous,' he explained.

A good deal of attention was also devoted to the cooling system, with a similar emphasis on making sure that it remained efficient when the car was sideways. Stevens was just as confident that the roof vent was a genuinely useful aid to cockpit ventilation – which isn't always the case – yet didn't disrupt airflow to the rear wing.

The bodyshell aside, most of the alterations were a matter of detail. There were new crossmembers and a new steering rack, a new dashboard and repositioned switchgear to improve weight distribution, a bigger petrol tank that generally obviated the need for an auxiliary tank in the boot and a modified exhaust allied to better cockpit insulation, to reduce temperatures inside the car. A revised transaxle casing cured the output flange's tendency to leak on the turbo side. Lighter suspension components helped save some of the extra weight of the bodyshell. While no internal changes to the engine were homologated, the ECU was remapped.

Lapworth estimated that the switch was as time-consuming as the process of creating the P2000, simply because of the need to make panel tooling and to restock spares. It had been wise to split the job in two.

Results soon suggested that his public faith in the car had been a touch misplaced. The truth was that the new bodyshell was heavier – naturally enough, when the car was 65mm longer – and initially, it was all Prodrive could do to stand still.

The longer nose gave a little more space, but under the bonnet the 2001 car – the S7 in Prodrive terms – bore a close resemblance to its immediate predecessor.

The interior was new, pushing the 2000 trend a little further. More switches were moved to the centre console, behind the handbrake, to improve weight distribution.

'For the first six months, I would have preferred to stay with the year 2000 car,' Burns admitted. 'I remember when I first got in the car – drove from Andorra, Monte test – I got in it and just said, "There's something wrong with that engine. It's like 30 horsepower down." It was shocking, really shocking. A couple of engineers said, "It feels different, because of the delivery."

'"No, it easily feels like 20–30 horsepower down." And it was: in Monte Carlo and Sweden it was, and they found a problem with the mapping, and from then on it was still not the best engine but it was more like it. You know when you get in the car whether it's going to be a good 'un or not, and that was one that didn't feel like it would be, straight away. But it turned into one. By halfway through the year it was back up there.

'It was very unreliable as well. At the end of the year, it was faultless, but by that time Paul Howarth was getting his fingers into things a lot better and the motivation definitely powered ahead towards the end of the year.'

Howarth had joined Prodrive from Cobra Motorsport in 1989 and spent many of the intervening years on the customer side of the business, running drivers such as Bertie Fisher and Freddy Dor. By the time he was appointed Operations Manager and put in charge of the workshop in the middle of the year, he was sorely needed.

The engine problem wasn't fully evident on the Monte, in fact, but only because all three cars retired embarrassingly early thanks chiefly to a rare but exasperating failure, a faulty batch of coils.

Burns salvaged 16th on the Swedish, setting a string of fastest stage times following a lengthy visit to a snowbank. It was one of the colder years of recent times, the mechanics fitting an extra heater after he complained that frosted side windows made it difficult to see round corners. He made do with fourth in Portugal (one of a number of rallies when yet more electronic and hydraulic glitches affected the gearbox) and seventh in Catalonia.

His teammates were doing no better. Sensing that Kankkunen was nearing the end of his career, Prodrive had snapped up two of the sport's rising stars late in 2000. The intention was that Petter Solberg (who was prised from Ford's grasp after a sulphurous contractual battle) and Markko Märtin would be joint number-two drivers. In fact, only Solberg had a contract for a full season, while it had also been agreed that Japan's leading driver, Toshihiro Arai, would drive a works car on a regular basis.

Poor Märtin was on his third rally with Subaru before he got as far as the third stage (his P2000's transmission failed after two stages in Australia, while his Monte coil expired before the first stage) and although he finished 12th on the Swedish, after stopping to change a puncture, his programme was mercilessly pruned as it became apparent that the team had its back to the wall. Fifth in Finland was one of the few highlights.

Solberg's form dissolved as soon as he changed manufacturers, partly because he was still coming to terms with his acrid departure from Ford, and partly because, as an ex-rallycross driver, he was still adapting to pace notes; five of his first seven rallies in Subarus ended in accidents. His engaging habit of apologising every time he crashed a car threatened to become routine.

All this certainly added to the strain, but it was Burns's inability to look like winning that created the most pressure. As a championship force, Subaru seemed spent – and to the outside world it looked all the worse, because it gave the impression that the new production car was inferior. Burns was second twice in a month, in Argentina and then Cyprus, but struggled to match Colin McRae. Solberg gave a hint of his potential with second on the

Acropolis, but it was another frustrating week, for Märtin broke the suspension when going well and Burns dropped out of a strong third near the end when he skidded over a bank for some minutes, confused by his own mid-stage signalling crew. To compound the damage, he retired shortly afterwards with a snapped propshaft.

Burns predicted that the Safari was the last roll of the dice. If he didn't finish well in Kenya, his championship bid would be as good as over. He retired on the first section with broken suspension, a similar failure later halting Arai, while Solberg was forced out with a wrecked wheel bearing. Burns was 25 points behind the resurgent Mäkinen with six rallies to run. Shortly afterwards, a disenchanted Loriaux left Prodrive for Ford's team, M-Sport. It was interpreted as the ultimate proof that the WRC2001 was a sow's ear.

Prodrive responded with its second reorganisation in seven months. In addition to transferring Howarth back to the works team, George Donaldson was recruited from Mitsubishi to fulfil the new role of Sporting Director, although he also took on much of the task hitherto performed by the team's departing, long-serving Team Manager, John Spiller.

The 2001 car wasn't at its best on asphalt, and in any case Sanremo was never one of Markko Märtin's happiest rallies in the earlier stages of his career.

Toshihiro Arai followed his Team's Cup triumph with sporadic works appearances in 2001, tackling Australia with characteristic gusto.

Although he couldn't quite match Marcus Grönholm, second place in Australia brought Richard Burns within striking distance of the World Championship.

Prodrive could shuffle the deckchairs – bring in new ones even – but compared to free-spending rivals, it looked no more likely to revive a championship assault than to refloat the *Titanic*. Yet in September, Lapworth appeared genuinely surprised that anyone should see the changes as crisis management.

'It's no use pretending that we could throw money at it, like Peugeot or Ford seem to be able to, but that isn't the only way,' he said. 'People often compare motorsport with warfare, don't they? Now, there are certain types of warfare to which the regular army is suited and certain battles are like the Somme where you need cannon fodder, and some aspects of warfare are much more suited to the SAS, where you only need a few people and some very clever tactics, and you can go in and achieve your objective.

'Now, I think that the World Rally Championship is more biased towards the kind of SAS campaign than it is towards First World War trench warfare, and therefore I

think that an organisation that is well-focused with an adequate budget can do extremely well. If Ford and Peugeot want to throw money at doing a Lancia and buying up the top four drivers in the world, then we will struggle, but teams like us and Mitsubishi, who have done very well over the last few years with a one-driver strategy, will still be able to do well by our SAS approach, by focusing on one driver, by focusing on young drivers – Colin came out of this kind of strategy don't forget, and won a World Championship. We think that is a perfectly valid strategy.'

By then, Burns was drawing precisely the opposite conclusion. As the team redoubled its efforts to make him World Champion, he entered final negotiations to join Peugeot.

Four months after that disastrous Safari, Lapworth was entitled to feel vindicated. When Burns and Reid clambered on to their Impreza's bonnet at the end of the Rally of Great Britain, they saluted the crowd as World Champions. Reorganisation and

unflinching determination had been rewarded.

'It was strange: the aim I set myself in the middle of 2001 was to get more points than Marcus, because if I was going to that team, to Peugeot, I wanted to go there ahead and that motivation won us the World Championship, because I think to aim to win the World Championship after Safari would have been deemed a little bit ridiculous at the time.

'There were a lot of meetings after Safari to establish how we could make sure we won, because we'd experienced quite a lot of finger trouble, but from then on absolutely everything was thrown into it to try to win the championship. And it worked: everything was triple-checked – absolutely everything by all accounts – and I think Prodrive probably learnt a hell of a lot in that respect as well. They'd seen how much effort you have to put in,' Burns suggested.

It was more than strange; it bordered on the miraculous. Burns faltered twice,

Once Margam's Gothic battlements were within range, Richard Burns was all but sure of second place on the Rally of Great Britain and the 2001 World Championship.

The moment that he had scarcely dared to believe possible: Richard Burns savours becoming World Champion.

crashing on the first stage at Sanremo – never one of his better rallies – and clattering his Impreza into a rockface in Corsica. Solberg and Märtin were ordered to slow near the end to give him two more places and two more points.

Yet he came to terms with the pressure better than any of his rivals. There has never been a season quite like it. It's rare for as many as eight drivers to win World Championship rallies in a year, but unprecedented that none should succeed on a consistent basis. Grönholm, Mäkinen and McRae won three times each, whereas Burns managed a solitary success in New Zealand, when Donaldson's ability to add under pressure proved superior to Peugeot's. Every leading driver had slowed on the stage that would dictate the starting order the next day, anxious to avoid running first. Thanks to Donaldson, Burns secured a more favourable position for the long, gravel-strewn leg north of Auckland, whereas Peugeot miscalculated Grönholm's 'ideal' time. New regulations have since stipulated that the leading crews start in reverse order for the second and third legs, removing the incentive for slowing tactically to drop places and gain more advantageous running positions on dry rallies.

Even Burns couldn't quite believe that every one of his rivals would crumble. It

wasn't until he finished second to Grönholm on the penultimate rally in Australia that he dared to dream that he might become champion.

He benefited from McRae's failure to arrive on time for a newly introduced ceremony in Australia, in which drivers chose their restart positions. It cost the Ford driver at least a place and raised the stakes considerably on the Rally GB. When McRae cut a corner and rolled on SS4, Burns was content to settle for third. It would have been insanely greedy to chase anything more. There was no arguing with the outcome, no denying that the car that had seemed such a liability had done him proud.

To cap an outlandish season, the championship was barely celebrated: within days, Subaru and Prodrive opened High Court proceedings in London to prevent the new World Champion from moving to Peugeot, claiming breach of contract and US$10,000,000 compensation. The matter was somewhat complicated in that the team had signed none other than Mäkinen in October and proclaimed him as the ideal replacement. Business and personal relationships were also dragged into the affair and they suffered before a settlement was reached out of court, after which Burns and Subaru went their separate ways.

Peugeot therefore started 2002 aiming for its third successive World Championship for Manufacturers with the champion drivers for the previous two years, backed up by Panizzi and the Finn, Harri Rovanperä, a quartet reputed to cost €17,000,000 per year. Burns maintained that the move had nothing to do with his salary, but something to do with money nevertheless. Peugeot ran four test cars when Subaru ran one. The attraction was a true works team, operated with a disregard for the law of diminishing returns that Lancia would have applauded and possibly envied.

Peugeot was selling over 2,000,000 vehicles per year, whereas Subaru sold in excess of 500,000; even if the Japanese firm devoted twice as much per car sold to rallying, it would struggle to match Peugeot's spending power. It had competed comfortably when budgets were around £20,000,000 per season in the mid-1990s. The environment had become a good deal less comfortable and Subaru therefore reappraised the programme for 2002. Prodrive was in no sense a pauper's team, however. As a four-times World Champion, Mäkinen naturally commanded a multi-million-pound retainer, and Solberg was well-rewarded too. Not for the first time, it was concluded that extra cars were more trouble than they were worth. Märtin was therefore released and Arai concentrated largely on the cheaper Group N production category.

Mäkinen wasted no time in justifying his fee. While Burns struggled to master the 206, the Finn revelled in the Impreza and became the first driver to win the Monte Carlo Rally four years running. It wasn't an entirely clear-cut victory, as the Frenchman, Sébastien Loeb, was in front when he was penalised two minutes for an illegal tyre change. As Citroën protested, the penalty was suspended and he 'won' the rally on the day, gaining much of the kudos. Citroën withdrew its appeal the following week, before an FIA hearing that might conceivably have increased the punishment. Whether Loeb would have held off Mäkinen in a straight fight is impossible to judge. Assuming that the penalty would be reapplied, Mäkinen had made no attempt to close the gap in the final leg, to his lasting regret; his tactics are an overlooked element in many partisan accounts of the rally.

The WRC2001's period of active service closed disappointingly with two engine failures on the Swedish, but the design's capabilities in all conditions were underlined when the WRC2002 appeared in Corsica. Peugeot swept the board in the end, but in the damp opening stages, both Mäkinen and Solberg threw the 206 flotilla on the defensive, prompting Panizzi to remark that the Subaru was the best Tarmac car. Both works Imprezas left the road, unfortunately, Solberg salvaging fifth, while Mäkinen retired at once, minus a wheel.

The WRC2002 had been unveiled without

fanfare, for the good reason that there wasn't much to trumpet. It looked near-identical (the front splitter was the only body panel to be redesigned, on the basis that the original had proved too susceptible to damage) and while the alterations under the skin were more extensive, it was possible to convert a 2001 car to the latest specification in half a day. The flywheel, exhaust manifolds and turbocharger were all new, along with the steering column.

The limited extent of the modifications

Petter Solberg carried the fight to the opposition, but couldn't ultimately hold off the phalanx of Peugeots in Corsica.

Some you lose: Tommi Mäkinen might easily have taken a fourth Argentine victory if it wasn't for a colossal accident near the finish.

didn't altogether explain why reliability had improved and continued to improve. In Burns's words, Howarth calls a spade a spade and the Lancastrian (subsequently promoted to Operations Director) maintained that the key to reliability had been new, vigorously implemented procedures rather than a drastic technical overhaul.

'I think from a customer background, when you're dealing with customers all the time, you have to deliver a 100% reliable package and the quality has to be bespoke,' he said. 'It has to be the best quality available. So maybe in a customer environment you do focus on quality. That is key. Customers don't give you any leeway: even if you've got a technical problem on an event, it's much harder to explain, so on the customer side, we'd probably developed different processes and more rigorous build standards.

'The factory cars were built to a very high standard, but we were doing more rallies and you do more rallies, you build more cars. You build more cars, different people build the cars, so you need to have more structure. You can't just get back from an event and a load of people start building the cars. A lot of the changes we did in the operation were more detailed planning, more structuring, more training, more rigorous, next-level-again of sign-off and that's probably nobody's fault. It's just the technical standards – the integrity – of the car had changed that much, you had to have a different approach. The gearbox procedure alone to shake the transmission down was probably two hours longer than it used to be to shake the car down from two years before. There was an emphasis on having to run all the parts on the shakedowns. You don't need to run the parts if you've got proper build procedures.'

The Legacy had seemed complicated compared to an M3, but the WRC99 had taken sophistication to new levels with its semi-automatic gearbox, which required more advanced electronics and hydraulics, running at higher pressure. The process had advanced another step with the P2000. The resultant niggles stemmed partly from its greater complexity and partly from staff changes, but Howarth is insistent that there was nothing wrong with the basic design.

'Christian [Loriaux] built a very fast and reliable car. Everyone said he made it fragile. The car wasn't fragile at all. It was more in the processes, things like a transmission problem in the hydraulics, you can always trace it back to poor assembly or you need a higher-quality assembly. There's normally a reason. If you look back at all the problems we had, that's normally the case,' Howarth said.

Opposite: *Tommi Mäkinen's Monte Carlo Rally record exhausts superlatives. In 2002, he completed his fourth successive win on his first rally for Subaru.*

When Petter Solberg is involved, it takes three to tango.

The 2002 Rally GB might easily have gone either way, but Petter Solberg rose to the occasion to win a duel with his erstwhile teammate Markko Märtin.

The hydraulics in particular had demanded new workshop techniques. Prodrive's engineers had been driven to distraction by gearbox faults, which persisted into 2001, two years after its launch. Sometimes, brand new parts seemed to be the worst. It subsequently emerged that water

It's always a team effort. Petter Solberg paid due tribute to his co-driver Phil Mills and the rest of the team after taking his first World Championship rally.

occasionally found its way in at the assembly stage, as a result of painstaking attempts to make sure that the parts were 'clean'. With small, sensitive Moog valves controlling key functions, microns mattered and 'clean' took on a new meaning.

Mäkinen was unlucky not to claim another victory in Argentina, when he was hot on Grönholm's heels and a long way in front of anyone else until he had an enormous accident at the end of one of the final stages. Grönholm's chances of finishing had already been called into question by an allegation of illegal servicing. He was thrown out at the finish, making Burns the victor until it emerged that his Peugeot's flywheel was underweight, turning Sainz into the third and final winner. Solberg, whose inexperience of a tricky rally had shown somewhat, ultimately finished second.

Occasional experiments with other drivers were not a success. Mäkinen was the only member of a four-car team to finish the Deutschland, taking a distant seventh, whereas Arai was sidelined by a broken gearbox and the Austrian, Achim Mörtl, floundered on his first run in a works car and crashed. Solberg also crashed heavily.

But as the Norwegian gained experience

and confidence, he gradually became the pacesetter. It helped that he knew the car better than Mäkinen, who struggled to explain what he wanted from a somewhat different car after years of a comfortable and familiar set-up at Mitsubishi. Initially, it was assumed that he wanted a car with a tendency towards understeer, much like Solberg. It turned out that a bias towards oversteer – along the same lines, albeit not as pronounced as Burns or McRae – was much more appropriate.

If there was a watershed, it came in Finland. Mäkinen had won the rally five times in a row in the 1990s and was brought up within a few miles of the stages. Nevertheless, it was Solberg, not quite able to match Burns, who came third, while his Finnish teammate was fifth. Yet, although the Imprezas were in the top three on three successive rallies in the closing months of the season, vanquishing the 206s appeared beyond them. The faster the rally, the greater the deficit, prompting Solberg to suggest that the flat-four was lagging behind other cars' engines.

If it wasn't for a hydraulic problem and then a momentary lapse of concentration at one of the best-known hazards in British

rallying, Deer's Leap, Grönholm would surely have taken the Rally GB too. Once the Finn's 206 had been reduced to a crumpled wreck on the Epynt Ranges, an entirely new prospect opened: the rally would be won either by Solberg or by his erstwhile teammate, Märtin.

There was nothing to choose between them as the final leg began, Märtin leading by 1.6 seconds. Indeed, the odds might be said to have favoured the Estonian, who had been the quicker by 11 seconds on the longest stage of the second leg, Resolfen. It was the first stage of the last day and therefore a vital chance to seize the initiative. Solberg rose to the occasion, gaining 21.9 seconds. While the Norwegian, with characteristic exuberance, conducted an impromptu victor's press conference from the roof of his winning car, Märtin could only admit that he had been too cautious in the fog.

It was an emotional success, the climax of a tumultuous year that had dealt out frustration and disappointment in generous measures. There were no championships to celebrate, but Subaru had unquestionably found a driver to follow in the footsteps of Sainz, McRae and Burns.

Toshihiro Arai walked away with the 2002 Japanese Alpine Rally, an all-asphalt event north of Tokyo, leading throughout in a works Impreza.

6 Sharpening the act

The 2003 season brought a fresh look and a fresh strategy. Subaru responded to the wounding criticism of the Impreza's appearance with a restyle, and Prodrive had simultaneously performed more extensive surgery beneath the skin. In the process, it had modified its old policy of redesigning the car every three years in favour of a more piecemeal approach.

'There's been a subtle shift in the way we operate,' David Lapworth explained. 'What we're trying to do now is still have a three-year cycle – and it's not strict – but do a third of the car each year, so from year to year we have a different priority, and over three years the car will have been completely refreshed. There'll be virtually nothing left from a 2002 car. What we do, if you like, is shift the priorities from one year to the next, so you're not turning up with a completely new and unproven car.

'In terms of test and development, it helps us to focus on the areas that are important. You're not running the whole car and you're not in that area – and I'm making this up – where you're hampered in doing your suspension testing because your engine keeps breaking down. You're not testing the whole car all the time.'

He reckoned that around 25% of the parts used in the Monte Carlo Imprezas had been reworked. Externally, the eye was drawn to the longer, sleeker nose and the new rear aerofoil with its four vertical strakes. It was designed to improve downforce in yaw and was promptly nicknamed the chipcutter. New mirrors sat further away from the doors, their slender stalks offering less resistance to airflow along the sides of the car. Prodrive claimed a worthwhile improvement in downforce from the changes, albeit not sufficient to demand new suspension settings.

Under the bonnet, FHI had provided a new turbo which was mated to new exhaust manifolds and a different intercooler. Although the 2003 version of the Impreza STi had an even bigger bonnet scoop, this did not find its way on to the WR Car, which took the less potent WRX as the basis for homologation. Prodrive and Subaru go to some lengths to accentuate the visual similarities between road and rally cars, but as the WR Car had a front-mounted intercooler, the bigger scoop would if anything have been a hindrance. The 2003 car also had a new, stiffer rollcage.

It was a cautious revision of the 2002 design in most respects, but a world away from the Impreza that had first appeared in Finland almost ten years previously. The original layout – a longitudinal boxer engine, a transaxle and MacPherson strut suspension – had stood the test of time admirably, but a decade's worth of progress and new regulations had brought a gradual transformation.

'In '93 and '94, it was probably taking two blokes three weeks to build a car,' Nigel Riddle explained. 'That wouldn't have included assembling the gearbox, assembling the engine, assembling the wiring loom. Three weeks would probably have had them on the ground, but it was a different business then; you put a lot more of your own bits together. You built your own suspension – that sort of stuff – and if you were given a

While his rivals wilted, Petter Solberg flourished in the enervating heat, endless corners, constant dust and rugged terrain, taking a convincing Cyprus victory in 2003.

month, that was probably quite nice. When we were busy, but didn't have that many people, it would invariably be one guy given the job to build Sweden cars, and he would probably start on one in January and work on his own until everybody got back from Monte Carlo, and then he'd have somebody with him for a couple of weeks to finish it. What were we operating? Even in that sort of time, I don't expect there was more than 150 of us here, mostly doing the rally as opposed to anything else then. But we were still pretty small for what we were trying to do. In the workshop we had 25–30 – not that many at all. In those days, I would have said 240–250 hours. It's probably the best part of double that now.

'Those bloody things are just so much more complicated. Hugely complicated: a hell of a lot more plumbing, and then over the years your standards get higher and higher and higher. It's a lot more putting on sub-assemblies, but then putting on sub-assemblies is quite a job. The set-up's half a day and fitting out the interior of these things is just bordering on the barking mad really, where everybody wants their telephone in such and such a place, and their screen angled at such and such an angle, and they want this and they want that, and one wants this button on the steering wheel and one doesn't; loads of that sort of stuff.

'I mean now, the lads probably sit down here for the best part of a day after the car's built, while it's still on stands, while they go through systems checks and all the bloody values until they get to the point where they're pressing the button and saying, "This is now really fit to drive"; Certainly half a day. Which is a bit like Formula 1, isn't it? Basically, no different. We're a bit more tolerant to conditions than they are, but most of the systems are exactly the same.'

In fact, the Monte Carlo cars were by no means the last word in 2003 Imprezas. The FIA will homologate – a precise translation from the French in which motorsport regulations were originally written, to 'approve' in short – one WR Car per manufacturer per year. However, there is abundant scope for significant modification which either doesn't require homologation or can be approved as a 'variant option'. Dampers belong to the former category and therefore one of the most far-reaching improvements to the 2003 Impreza didn't arrive until May, when the team ended its long-standing relationship with Bilstein and switched to Sachs.

Bilstein was once a near-universal supplier to works rally teams, but the German company's gas-filled dampers came to seem primitive as other manufacturers began experimenting with alternatives that had remote reservoirs and offered a greater range of adjustment. Prodrive had responded by developing its own hybrid dampers, assembled and increasingly developed at Banbury along Bilstein principles, with a single remote reservoir per damper. Even these were no longer deemed suitable and the Sachs units, which offered separate high- and low-speed adjustment of bump and rebound settings, were therefore introduced for Argentina.

They were a mixed blessing at first. There was no arguing with the theory, but Solberg in particular felt they needed further tuning and was also hampered by a curious and alarming tendency for the car to spear to the left under braking; he finished fifth, having rolled once and careered into a ditch later on at high speed. The discussions with his engineer, Pierre-Yves Genon – like the damper adjustments – were endless.

If Argentina provoked the thought that a little more testing would have done no harm, there was no questioning the worth of the change within a few weeks, but a much more radical suspension experiment came close to undermining Solberg's title hopes at a critical point in the season. If it had worked, the 'active' Impreza might have taken its place in motorsport history alongside cars such as the Chaparral 2J or the Brabham BT46B fan car. Instead, it lasted less than one day of one event and the 2005 ban on active suspension cut short further development.

The possibilities were tantalising. Pirelli's best dry-weather Tarmac tyres were reckoned to be almost a second per mile slower than Michelin's. As three of the last four rounds of the 2003 World Championship were on asphalt, Solberg risked being trampled in the rush for the title. Active suspension might just turn the tide. Such systems had never previously been used in rallying, because the environment was too demanding for the available level of technology – or at least outside the scope of a rally team's budget. A number of manufacturers had experimented with such systems, though, and it's an indication of their complexity that Prodrive had started doing so as long ago as the 1980s on BMWs.

By late 2003, fitting a new suspension system to the Impreza was deemed to be worth the gamble. It had covered 3,000 miles in the previous six months and had been tested both at MIRA and at the demanding Alès circuit in the south of France. It was a calculated risk and the new set-up was, therefore, given to Solberg alone for the Sanremo Rally. Lapworth was adamant, too, that it wasn't a truly active system, on the

basis that it reacted to road conditions and had much the same effect as Peugeot's active, hydraulically actuated anti-roll bars.

'It's not active suspension. It's a roll control system. The ride is still controlled by the springs and dampers. The system only deals with roll and pitch. You can keep the body flatter – that's where most of the advantage comes from. The tyres sit flat on the road,' he said.

He conceded that elements of the system were closed-loop – generally regarded as a defining characteristic of an active system – and that as it 'added energy' to the suspension, it would be banned under 2005 rules.

The Sanremo car did away with anti-roll bars, relying on the old Bilstein struts and an extra hydraulic reservoir per damper, linked to accumulators and a hydraulic pump running at a pressure of 140–150bar. It reacted to a variety of inputs, including yaw, lateral and longitudinal g, and relied on a new, more advanced ECU made by TAG. Despite being more softly sprung, it sat

Subaru's 2003 season began promisingly, but disappointment soon followed. Petter Solberg was running strongly on the Monte until he hit a bridge.

noticeably lower than a conventional Impreza and, rather like a hydropneumatic Citroën, it raised itself when the engine was switched on as hydraulic pressure climbed.

Solberg had been eager to use it for some time, but his morale was dented as early as the shakedown, when the best Michelin runners were significantly quicker in the closing minutes; it was a harbinger of what was to come.

Prodrive reckoned the new suspension added 25 kilos and cost 2bhp. Rivals suggested that 20bhp would be closer to the mark, and clearly there was a fuel consumption penalty. Scarcely two miles from the final service area of the day in Imperia, Solberg coasted to a halt, out of petrol and out of the rally. It appeared that he was the victim of an oversight in programming fuel consumption into the new computer, but the fact that he was no higher than eighth, two minutes behind the leader, ensured that the old suspension was reinstated a fortnight later in Corsica.

By Sanremo, Solberg had had a great deal to lose, which spoke volumes for the team's

and the driver's resilience after a distinctly uneven start to the season. The Imprezas were instantly on the pace on the Monte, but both were off the road before the end of the first leg, Solberg managing two excursions in as many stages.

He couldn't get anywhere near Mäkinen on the Swedish. In one of his finest drives for the team, the Finn gave Grönholm a run for his money, comfortably beating Burns to take a worthy second. Solberg was out of sorts on snow – a puzzling state of affairs for someone born 60 degrees from the Equator, but a reflection of his background in rallycross rather than rallying – and he made do with sixth, confessing that he had something to learn.

Mäkinen salvaged eighth and a solitary point from Turkey in the end, having wrecked the suspension on a rally every bit as rough as the Acropolis. It should accordingly have been tailor-made for the Imprezas, as Solberg had hinted until he slithered wide, clouted a rock and broke a steering arm on the fourth stage. The car was almost unmarked, but out of the rally.

The 2003 Swedish was one of Tommi Mäkinen's finest drives for Subaru, a gutsy performance earning second place.

It hadn't turned the season into a rearguard action by any means, but by Argentina, Solberg was painfully conscious that he had to score consistently and that if he was to stand any chance of winning the championship, he would have to pick his moments carefully. It seemed a very tall order indeed when Peugeot was very much in command: Grönholm flattened all opposition to take three of the first five rallies, while Burns's flawless consistency kept him at the head of the points table. Solberg was convinced that the WRC2003's engine was its weak link, costing him points in New Zealand (one of the fastest rallies in the series) and at altitude in Argentina, one of the highest.

He didn't mind dwelling on the engine's deficiencies in public, either, but this wasn't the whingeing of an over-indulged sportsman. An articulate and intelligent man, he had learnt that endless grumbling in public is bad for morale and put him in the wrong frame of mind as well. The comments about the engine were a calculated attempt to spur the engineers into a response.

In other respects, Solberg's praise for the team was unstinting. In the later months of the season he became more than a driver. He had demonstrated his faith in Subaru by signing a new, long-term contract as early as May, turning down enquiries from the French manufacturers, and this commitment to the team was combined with a new composure at the wheel. As a result, he became one of its leaders, gaining some of the inspirational quality that McRae had had in the 1990s.

There is a view within Prodrive that Solberg is the most gifted driver the team has ever had. For all his self-confidence, it took the Norwegian a while to come to terms with his ability, and he has confessed that there have been rallies he threw away by trying too hard, too soon. In the latter part of 2003, he developed the knack of succeeding by pacing himself. His first victory of the year, in Cyprus, was the result that the Impreza ought to have achieved from the outset on such a rough and twisty event. It was a model victory, a beautifully judged drive in the Troodos Mountains complemented by a

The low centre of gravity permitted by a horizontally opposed engine is perfectly illustrated by this shot of a 2003 engine.

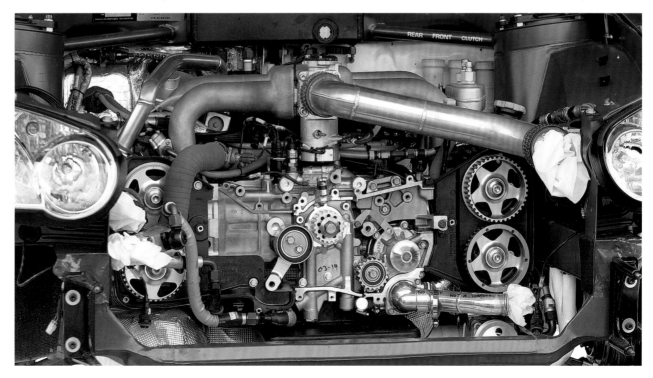

consistently well-drilled performance from the mechanics baking in ferocious heat on Limassol's docks.

By then, he at last had the car he wanted. While he had given the appearance of turning Argentina into a test session, the Sachs shock absorbers were in fact the ultimate refinement, completing the adaptation from the car that Burns or McRae would have recognised to the car that Solberg wanted. Oversteer hasn't become a thing of the past by any means, but Solberg belongs to a new generation of drivers who like their cars to be neutral. The P2000 that Burns had adored and Kankkunen had admired, Solberg had tolerated at best.

'It was very easy to drive – it was too easy! For me, when a car is so easy to drive and you can just play with it and go sideways, it's really a back-wheel-drive car. It didn't feel like any car I'd driven, because it was so back-wheel drive. I didn't struggle to drive it, because that was easy, but to get the times with it for me, who was used to a completely different driving style, it was difficult,' he said.

However, this was only one of his difficulties. Persuading Prodrive that he wanted a more neutral car – in essence, a racing car for the forests – set off a prolonged struggle. Adjusting a car to driver preference made sense, but giving the Norwegian what he said he wanted flew in the face of precedent. He wanted a precision that didn't accord with an environment with thousands of different corners and a set-up that seemed just as inappropriate when conditions were often unpredictable and treacherous.

Early in 2004, Solberg joked that he drove Lapworth bald, but he got his way.

'If you talk to David about it, he took his hands and almost took all his hair off his head: "Petter, anybody else can drive it – Colin and Richard."

'"Yeah, but I'm not that type of driver! I'm a perfectionist. I want everything to be neutral. I don't want to have any oversteer. I want to have a little bit understeer. Off and on throttle I want the car to be neutral."

'He said, "Yeah, but that's how it is."

'"Yeah, you have to do something with it!" I said, "If I am going to be the best."

'"Rallying you don't have to be so perfectionist, because everything is changing all the time."

'But I said, "David, you know, I want to have it differently," and now, the last two years, I am happy. They have done a lot of changes with the car and diffs, and damping is completely different. If you look at the rates on the damping you would not recognise the car at all.'

To Solberg's mind, the centre and rear differentials had been doing far too much of the work. Hydraulic pressure in the front differential has been increased, but in response the engineers have also revised the suspension geometry, softened the dampers' bump and rebound settings to enhance stability at high speed and retuned the engine, seeking extra torque at lower revs rather than high-rev power. Pirelli has had to adapt its tyres to suit.

Solberg cheerfully concedes that it is an inherently risky approach; the mind boggles how he would cope if the Rally GB still had a secret route.

'It is more difficult to drive, it is a more dangerous way to drive, but it is quicker,' he said.

Lapworth agrees that he took some persuading, acknowledges that it works for the Norwegian, but suspects that oversteer won't fade into history and that in particularly treacherous conditions, a neutral car won't be quite as quick.

In Australia, Solberg maintained that he didn't live especially dangerously, yet he won a long, tense duel with Loeb. While he was thrilled, it was nothing compared to his delight at overhauling Burns for second on the last stage in Finland, by 1.8 seconds.

'I didn't want to lead and take ten seconds lead or something,' he said confidently at the finish in Australia. 'I hate it, seriously. I need the adrenalin, I need the hard competition so I can come to the next level to beat them like I did today. It was meant to be to do a mistake on the second stage today. It was almost, you

shouldn't be leading after the second stage, you have to do it close to the finish! Also the weather helped me a little bit, I think, because the tyres and the car and me works better on really difficult conditions. I can go more harder than I did today, actually.'

Damp conditions had helped, but so had a marginally more twisty route than in previous years. Solberg loves slow rallies in any case, but again, he stressed that they suited the engine.

Sanremo threatened to undo all the progress made. It wasn't just that the 'roll control' system hadn't paid off, but the demoralising thought that the conventional car wouldn't do much better on dry asphalt.

After the shakedown, there was a distinct possibility that Solberg wouldn't take part in the Tour of Corsica at all. He had been outwitted by a patch of gravel, skated wide and chopped a telegraph pole in two. The impact deprived a neighbouring village of electricity and damaged the Impreza so badly that the team considered flying in a replacement. The stewards refused to permit the car swap, as the original had already

been scrutineered. After considering Mäkinen's generous offer to withdraw and offer his car, the team embarked on the much more laborious process of rebuilding the Norwegian's.

Although the C-post on the driver's side had taken the brunt of the impact, one front chassis leg was an inch out of line, the other two inches. The mechanics found a jig in a nearby garage and worked through the night to straighten it. The repair wasn't perfect but it was sound enough, and by dawn the car was running. The telltale ripples couldn't be entirely eradicated, but the car's appearance was very much a secondary consideration. Simon Steele, one of the old hands, bravely suggested that it was a good omen, recalling that Prodrive had won its first World Championship rally after Béguin had crashed his BMW testing in Corsica in 1987. Another member of the team reflected that the biggest question concerned the driver, not the car: how much harm had the crash done to his confidence? In comparison, a few millimetres in the chassis alignment paled into insignificance.

Years of development went unrewarded when the 'active' Impreza appeared on the 2003 Sanremo Rally. It's little wonder that Petter Solberg looks uneasy as he contemplates a serious suspension problem.

Solberg's customary sparkle had deserted him. The alternative to the pole had been a towering drop. It had been a queasy reminder of the sport's dangers.

Sure enough, he was a distant eighth after the dry first leg, 43 seconds behind Loeb's Citroën and damage limitation looked to be very much the operative term. But the next morning it rained and instantly Solberg was on the pace. Despite a spin, he had rocketed up to third after two more stages, and when Loeb and Märtin spun, a wildly improbable victory became a distinct possibility. Steadily, Solberg reeled in François Duval's Focus and Carlos Sainz's Xsara, and that evening he led by 17.9 seconds. It was wet again on the Sunday and the unanswered question was no longer whether Solberg could win, but whether Duval could hold off Sainz.

It was one of the most extraordinary results in the rally's history – one of the most extraordinary in Subaru's, come to that – and, as Solberg was happy to acknowledge, a true team effort.

'When they said the car is too bad to repair, then my head started going round. You know, because I'm taking it so seriously

In Corsica, Petter Solberg's prospects took an instant turn for the worse. The left-hand side shows the result of the impact with a telegraph pole.

and I'm getting really upset about myself and I take it so hard, because I am a sportsman and I hating mistakes. Then David [Lapworth] said, "Last chance, we look at the car," and said, "OK we go for it, definitely." Safety first, that was the main thing. If it was not safe we would not have done it.

'I was nervous, I had a little bit of respect for what happened. It could have been much worse. It just kept my feet on the floor again and it kept me even more concentration. I just put even more effort in. After what the guys have done, I put even more in myself. I did just one mistake, which was having one spin, the whole rally. I lost 15 seconds there, that's all.

'Maybe the first start in the morning, my stomach was going around, but I don't think anybody is more happy than me now, for the mechanics. I think this is different. It's very, very personal things with the mechanics and everything. It's feelings into this victory, respect for what they have done for me and what could have happened. I am very proud, to come from where we was to come up to this shouldn't be possible.'

It rained again in Catalonia, but only on the last day. Never a profitable hunting ground for Subaru in recent times, even Solberg languished in tenth place after the first leg and ninth after the second. In the closing stages he was sometimes over a second per mile quicker than the opposition and he snatched fifth place at the last gasp: the result put him a point behind the joint championship leaders, Loeb and Sainz, and four ahead of Burns, but given past form on the Rally of Great Britain, he was generally considered to be the World Championship favourite.

There were all kinds of other factors to consider, too. Citroën was also locked in combat with Peugeot for the manufacturers' title, and Citroën Sport's Director, Guy Fréquelin, made it abundantly clear that that was the priority.

He was as good as his word. Peugeot had already been deprived of Burns, who was invalided out four days before the start of the rally when it emerged that he had a brain tumour. Within three stages, Grönholm wrecked his 206's steering and Citroën lost Sainz, who crashed after a succession of in-

car electrical fires linked to the onboard TV camera. As two Citroëns remained and both were needed at the finish, Loeb was ordered to let Solberg go.

It was something of an anticlimax, but in Fréquelin's view it made no difference to the final result. On Pirellis, in muddy Welsh forests, in a Subaru, Solberg would have been as good as unbeatable. It wasn't an easy victory: the Norwegian had felt the pressure as keenly as any of his rivals in the days before the start. There were occasional scares during the rally, too, notably when he damaged a steering link after hitting a hole a mile into the longest stage, Resolfen, on Saturday. Yet he increased his lead still further and, to round off a triumphant season, Mäkinen, sporting a pair of gold-coloured boots provided by the clothing sponsor, Alpinestars, outran McRae to take third on his final rally for the team.

It had been too close to call for most of the season. Yet although the one-point winning margin was proof that no one had dominated, Solberg prevailed rather as Burns had two years before: he had coped best with the pressure. It was a collective triumph in

Given a winding road, steady rain and an Impreza, Petter Solberg was in his element. His Corsican triumph was one of the least likely of Subaru's World Championship rally victories.

The motorhome isn't necessarily a place to relax and it isn't necessarily off limits, but it certainly gives the crews a chance to escape the limelight.

which the team had proved once more that it could fell much bigger, much better-funded opponents.

As Solberg's engineer, Genon, commented, 'It was a very close championship and at some point it didn't look too likely for us to win it. I still can't understand how we did! Sometimes it was other people's mistakes, but that's part of the job and as a team thing, if you win because of some other people's mistakes, whether it's driver or team mistakes or whatever, it means you haven't made these mistakes yourself and that's great. It's as much avoiding mistakes as doing fantastic things and there are a lot of ways to make mistakes in this game.'

It would have been asking a great deal to maintain such form into the new season, but Solberg didn't even try. Acutely conscious that he had done a much better job of squandering than scoring points on the opening rallies in previous years, he was content to bank safe finishes from the Monte and the Swedish, the 2003 car's final factory outings. A potentially costly excursion demoted him to a distant seventh on the former, but tuition from Mäkinen and a conscious effort to adopt a more aggressive technique earned him third on the latter –

and he might have done better still if it hadn't been for a faulty anti-lag system and a trip into the scenery during the second leg.

The team had become still more reliant on Solberg, as Mäkinen had been replaced by Mikko Hirvonen when it became clear that Burns would not be able to fulfil the contract agreed the previous August. Selecting a highly promising young Finn shouldn't have been a controversial choice, but it was, as Prodrive had been on the brink of agreeing terms with Colin McRae, only for negotiations to collapse in a welter of recriminations at the last minute. It was not the last indication that money was tight.

That wasn't apparent from the Impreza WRC2004's first appearance. Fourth and fifth places for Solberg and Hirvonen on the Rally Mexico in March didn't begin to do the car justice. Solberg was aggrieved but thrilled, regretful that he hadn't taken a victory that would have stood comparison with the WRC97's and P2000's first successes, scarcely able to believe that he might have won the rally by two and a half minutes.

At a glance, it would be difficult to tell a WRC2004 from its predecessor. In practice, a host of changes amounted to 'a big third', as

Lapworth put it. Under the direction of the new designer, Ed Wood, around half the car had been altered during a 14-month revitalisation.

Closer inspection revealed new radiator exit vents on each side of the front bumper. The intercooler had been re-angled (tilting forward, not back) along with the upper air intake apertures, while the rear aerofoil was new. The interior was also redesigned.

The changes were more obvious beneath the bonnet. The switch from FHI/GEMS to TAG electronics had been completed, indicated by an array of sensors clustered around the inlet manifold. It was a far cry from the system fitted to the Impreza 555 a decade previously. The 36 sensors had grown to 60, and three separate ECUs had been combined in a single TAG unit, with four 32-bit microprocessors. Both STi and GEMS continued to supply some components. The biggest advances were in speed, weight reduction and ease of operation. Calculations were performed more quickly, and new software, written by STi and Prodrive, improved engine control, which contributed to sharper response.

'We actually end up with about 120 channels on the data, because some of the channels are not reading the sensor, they're calculations made in the ECU on the status of something, for example the engine or some alarms, some fail codes, things that will give you a clue if there's anything wrong, and the other half of them are just sensors. It's a bit of work to make sure everything works,' Genon explained.

The new electronics were combined with less visible engine changes. The turbocharger's compressor and centre housing were new, fed by new exhaust manifolds, while a revised crankshaft and connecting rods saved a kilogramme. Development had been carried out jointly at Prodrive, by a team led by John Carey, Nick Dennis and Stéphane Girard, and by STi in Japan. Inevitably, power was still quoted at 300bhp, but torque – a less political and consequently more reliable measurement – has climbed markedly to 60 kilos/metre at 4,000rpm.

However, the bulk of the effort had been put into exploiting new bodyshell regulations. The FIA had authorised the most extensive regulation changes since the introduction of WR Cars, partly to reflect trends in road car design, partly to reduce costs. As they offered potential performance

For three days Petter Solberg's fans had followed his progress with rapt attention. The last stage of the Rally of Great Britain undammed a wave of pent-up emotion.

benefits as well, Subaru naturally seized the opportunity. Bodyshells must weigh at least 320 kilos, but front and rear wings can be changed from steel to plastic, while bonnet and boot lid can be changed for aluminium, and side and rear windows can be plastic. Minimum weights for bumpers and windscreens were imposed, too, to discourage the use of expensive, ultra-light materials.

The change involved a good deal of paperwork, as all parts removed had to be specified and weighed, but while the wings were lighter, Prodrive chose to make them from aluminium rather than carbon fibre. The weight saving wasn't as great, but it did allow the use of existing tooling, which saved money.

Cost influenced the bodyshell in other ways, too. In places, there was more use of reinforcement and double skinning than performance demanded. Wood and his colleagues had one eye on more stringent limits on servicing and a consequent need for

reliability, but the other on making sure that shells lasted longer. Yet another new rollcage contributed to a 15% increase in stiffness. The weight saving amounted to ten kilos, allowing more use of ballast to enhance weight distribution.

The effort to prune weight had been considerable. Unprecedented use was made of finite element analysis, both in the shell and suspension design.

'Most of it has evolved from practical experience,' Lapworth said. 'We've been running basically the same configuration of suspension for ten years now and every time you have a small accident, every time you have a heavy landing, you learn a little bit more about where the damage occurs, where the cracks start to occur first and so on, and most of the design has evolved that way. What we've done with this car, if you like, is closed the loop. We've still got that information, but we've also improved our modelling of it to feed back to a new design that incorporates the best of both worlds, so

The WRC2004's performance more than lived up to expectations. Only a minor electrical problem denied Petter Solberg victory in Mexico on its first appearance.

we've got all those benchmarks, we've got all that established customer practice, but we've put a lot more effort into the actual modelling of it, so that hopefully we've been able to achieve at least the strength of the old suspension, yet save quite a bit of weight.'

The 2004 car also gained a new pedal box and a new rear differential. Once again, it was an active, hydraulic design, with its own pump and a magnesium alloy casing, but it was an epicyclic type, made by Xtrac, and was intended to reduce friction.

Solberg promised that he had been biding his time, waiting for the first loose-surface rally of the season, and in Mexico, he was as good as his word. He was fastest on nine of the 15 stages, revelling in the car's superior torque and greater stability. There were some grounds for reserving judgement: the rally was new and run at unusually high altitude for a World Championship rally, one of the stages above Leon reaching 2,700 metres, with a consequently dramatic effect on engine performance. Nevertheless, many of

the stages were run at high average speeds – precisely the sort of terrain on which Solberg had felt the car had been weakest.

Lapworth reckoned that the WRC2004 had had the lengthiest, smoothest development phase of any recent Impreza and yet unfamiliarity helped turn Solberg's early lead into fourth. The road section between the last stage of the first leg and the service area was slackly timed and in common with most drivers, Solberg arrived early. He switched the car off while waiting, but killed the ignition, not the master switch. It wouldn't have mattered with the old electronic set-up – nor with the TAG system if the alternator hadn't gone sick on the run-in. Unfortunately, as the master switch was on, the ECU continued to download data and when it was time to enter service, the battery was too flat to turn the starter motor.

It still wouldn't have mattered if the time control had been on flat ground, but it was up a concrete ramp, and by the time Solberg

When a turbo restrictor stifles the capacity to flow air, every detail counts in the quest for power. The array of sensors were the visible evidence of the 2004 car's advanced TAG engine management system. Re-angling the intercooler had an aerodynamic function.

and Mills had heaved the car into the control, they were 40 seconds late. All was not lost, but they had had help in pushing the car and the stewards therefore imposed an additional five-minute penalty. A spectacular comeback turned 13th place into fourth, 3 minutes 14 seconds behind Markko Märtin's victorious Focus.

Team and driver were entitled to regard the Rally of New Zealand as vindication. After a long and draining battle with Marcus Grönholm, Solberg took one of the fastest rallies in the World Championship by just 5.9 seconds. The outcome had been as close as the winning margin suggested.

Pirelli's new KP tyre had been designed to cope with solidly founded dirt roads, but with a slightly more open tread pattern than the usual K to disperse loose gravel. The K would have been a better choice for an exceptionally dry and warm North Island autumn, but as it hadn't been nominated in advance, the rules forbade the team from using it. Solberg and Hirvonen therefore had to cope with squirming treads that robbed

them of badly needed precision at high speeds.

Solberg coped and led after each leg, but his lead became very precarious indeed when he struck a rock on the most formidable stage of the last leg, Whaanga Coast, which he swore had not been there during the recce. The impact damaged the suspension and wrecked the power steering. After five miles, he had conceded 20 seconds and pulled a chest muscle.

But Solberg is a master of close finishes, and Grönholm had lived dangerously throughout. He had tipped his 307 on its side when pulling away in the first leg and he made two decisive errors in the sprint for the line, overshooting on the first run at Whaanga Coast, then spinning when the handbrake jammed on the following stage. Solberg commented that the Peugeot was quicker in a straight line, but suggested that Grönholm's speed went hand in hand with his tendency to overcook things.

'I have been in so many fights that I really don't know if this was the toughest, but I

Petter Solberg was in masterly form in New Zealand, giving the Impreza WRC2004 its first win, but he was pressed hard by Marcus Grönholm.

was most afraid of the guy behind me, definitely, because he is very quick, I must say. It is going too quick sometimes, when you make mistakes. I knew it would be tough on some stages and there was no turning point at all. With the very high temperatures and stuff, I struggled,' he said.

Seven weeks later, the Norwegian turned from blond to bald when his head was shaved during a characteristically rumbustious post-Acropolis celebration. There was no arguing with the result and the 18-second winning margin over Loeb's Citroën might easily have been five times as great. Solberg had been relieved and a touch surprised to lose no more than half a minute when the brakes failed on the longest stage, and disgusted when he was docked 30 seconds by the stewards for attempting a handful of stages without mudflaps. Like most rally drivers, Solberg tends to regard mirrors, bumpers, and even lights, as optional extras; mudflaps naturally fall into the same category. It was a breach of the regulations, but not normally punished in such a manner.

Lighter and neater, each new Impreza cockpit takes sophistication and refinement a step further.

A successful rally car needs to combine sophistication with brute strength. As Petter Solberg discovered in Argentina, the WRC2004 had an unfortunate aversion to water.

By then, chinks in the 2004 Impreza's armour had begun to emerge. Solberg had eased his way into the lead from the start in Cyprus, despite three, run-flat punctures on one stage, only to pull up on the fourth stage with chronic overheating. On soft, badly cut-up stages, the front spoiler shovelled sand and grit into the radiator, sending the temperature gauge off the scale. The engine held, but Solberg lost four minutes on the stage and had conceded ten by the time his service crew were able to clean the radiator and make a grille to repel debris.

In Turkey and Argentina, more potential wins went begging, as water proved as destructive as sand. Taking fords at speed caused an astonishing amount of damage to body panels and ducting. Subsequent analysis revealed that water generated 2.5g as it surged through the front of the car. It could bend the bonnet so badly that the driver struggled to see over it. Even more seriously,

it wrecked carbon fibre ducting, blasting aside a flap designed to protect the air intake and entering the engine. Solberg retrieved third in Turkey, but after numerous mishaps in fords and a fire, the car failed to complete the first leg in Argentina.

The prototype had naturally been tested in water, but generally at some depth and consequently at low speeds. No one had imagined that fast, shallow crossings would be a problem – although speed didn't seem to be the overriding factor in Argentina, both drivers reporting trouble no matter what approach they took.

With a tight budget, it wasn't possible to test as much as the French teams, and this had an affect on both performance and reliability. As the pressure mounted, things went from bad to worse. Solberg was roused from his sickbed to compete in Finland and was doing better than expected when he slid off and broke the suspension. To add insult

It was a bruising, shocking experience at the time. Subsequently, Petter Solberg and Phil Mills paid tribute to the design of the car, having walked away from their Deutschland wreck. The data logger recorded five separate impacts in 5.7 seconds, the first at 75mph.

to injury, Hirvonen managed to crash on the shortest stage of the first leg and do considerable damage to both sides of the car.

In Germany, Solberg confessed that he was 'overdriving', desperate to keep up on Tarmac and paying the price in a savage encounter with the Baumholder military ranges' fearsome *Hinkelsteins*. Considering that they're designed to repel tanks, the Impreza withstood a series of violent impacts outstandingly well.

The World Championship had turned heavily in Loeb's favour, but Solberg's faith in the Impreza was undimmed. It had in some respects proved an unlucky car and in 2004, Subaru depended more than most of its rivals on one driver. Despite the setbacks, Solberg remained convinced that the car was a winner.

In Hokkaido, on Japan's first World Championship rally, Subaru could not have wished for a better demonstration of the Impreza WRC2004's capabilities. Solberg and Mills became the first crew to lead a World Championship qualifier throughout since Loeb won at Sanremo 11 months previously, and the car required nothing other than a set of brake discs, pads and

some precautionary maintenance of the water injection.

It was an utterly convincing performance, in which Solberg exceeded all reasonable expectations so soon after his German accident. It was a tense rally nonetheless, for Loeb pressed hard in the first leg, closing in during the afternoon when the Norwegian picked the wrong tyres. The boot was on the other foot the following morning and, after being crushed by 19 seconds on the 13th of the 27 stages, Loeb settled for second.

'It was such an important rally to win. As a single event, this is the most important rally that we've ever done, coming to Japan with Subaru,' a relieved, delighted Lapworth admitted at the finish.

Hirvonen displayed truly Finnish grit, taking seventh despite being towed off a stage when a hydraulic problem stranded him in neutral. To save weight, WRC2004s have no manual back-up gearlever, and after 30 minutes of unremitting graft, he found a ratio – a fine demonstration of his mechanical skills.

Solberg was thrilled, with the car, with the result and with the response from the local fans. It had been fun from start to finish.

The Mosel vineyards provide a picturesque backdrop for the Deutschland. Mikko Hirvonen threads his WRC2004 between the vines.

7 Evolution of the species

'It was so hot, because he'd punctured the radiator, and it was rattling and banging, and I thought as soon as he switched it off, "That will never, ever, ever start again." He'd pushed the whole engine and gearbox back, and he couldn't get second, fourth or sixth, because the gear lever was at the back of the hole, and there was one bloke with a hammer and chisel, chiselling on the back of the gear lever, so he could get enough travel on the gear lever, and he's trying to boot it with a sledgehammer and stuff, and by this time we've got some water in it and trying to start it, get it running, and it rattled like you wouldn't believe. You would never have thought it would have done another yard. But we got it running, trying to get some water in it and it's throwing it out, because it's boiling and it's red hot, chucking water out.

'And Johnny's battering the hole with a sledgehammer and he hit the gearlever, knocked it in gear, while about two or three of us are round the front trying to fasten it all back, and it lurched into gear ... knocked us all flying!

'But, eventually, it cooled down and quietened down; finished the gear lever job, so you could get all the gears, strapped bits of radiator into it, sumpguard – foam and tie wraps everywhere. But he got going, set off and he got to the stage with less than a minute.'

Steve Wilson, one of the mechanics sent flying, laughed at the memory. Raising write-offs from the dead is part of the appeal of being a rally mechanic – one of the main attractions to some – and, against all odds,

Colin McRae won the 1993 Rally of Malaysia despite wrapping his Legacy round a tree in a plantation. Driving skill was all very well, but the engine's appetite for punishment and his mechanics' resourcefulness were just as important.

Wilson – always self-employed, but so much a part of Prodrive for more than a decade that the usual description, 'mercenary', wouldn't begin to do him justice – accepts that the Malaysian resurrection is history, as far removed from rallying at its highest level now as completing a race without refuelling is from 21st-century Formula 1.

'There's no comparison these days, none whatsoever. I can appreciate that rallying did have to change and there was no way it could carry on the way it was. It was anti-social, dangerous – but I wouldn't have missed it for the world,' he said.

On a 21st-century rally, McRae would almost certainly have retired at the stage finish, because the engine would have seized within a handful of miles. He would have continued only if he had been lucky enough to have the crash within a short distance of the strictly rationed service locations permitted on major rallies.

Quite a few of the old faces are still to be found at Banbury, but the team has changed – not just in accordance with Subaru's wishes, not just because better ways of doing things are worked out with the passage of time, but to reflect the shifting nature of the sport. Indeed, constant change has become one of international rallying's abiding characteristics.

By 1999, personal manoeuvrability still counted for a good deal for a mechanic, but the appearance of the service point itself had become a consideration. Juha Kankkunen's Impreza is serviced on the seafront at Sanremo, next to a glossily painted team artic.

In 1993, servicing restrictions were minimal, if they existed at all. It was therefore routine for a works team to station an emergency service crew as close as possible to a special stage finish (just like the band who saved McRae's Legacy in Malaysia) in addition to a main service point close to the start of the next stage. Most of the resources were concentrated at the latter and, as a rule, the emergency point would be visited solely if the car wasn't capable of going any further under its own power. If the organisers happened to set up a time control or regroup between stages, that meant an additional service point. The idea was to service as close as possible to the time control or the stage to maximise repair time and, where appropriate, to improve the chances of making an accurate tyre choice.

Works teams routinely planned dozens of service points per rally, for which Prodrive had a well-drilled squad of mechanics who had learnt their trade on club rallies. Many

of them had competed themselves. The nucleus of a well-drilled team had been formed in the 1980s, and when the Subaru programme began it was principally the car that was found wanting, not the support operation.

As a rule, two mechanics travelled in each van, with support crews in estate cars – popularly, if unofficially, known as chase cars – and possibly in helicopters too. The headcount varied from rally to rally, but it would consist of at least 40 people on a World Championship event, rising to 60 or so on the Monte Carlo Rally and once to 72 on a Safari. Those events stood apart, the former, because the possibility of changeable conditions required extra weather and ice note crews to make a last-minute check of the stages, the latter thanks to the distances involved and the roughness of Kenya's back roads.

Employing roads open to normal traffic also made the Safari unique. As speeds climbed, aerial guidance became a feature –

Traditionally, speed and manoeuvrability were everything, for the service vans often covered a greater distance than the rally cars and any reasonably flat piece of ground would suffice.

Toyota and Nissan using aeroplanes to warn of oncoming traffic and stray animals in the 1980s. Inevitably, the next step was to resort to helicopters, which were more manoeuvrable; although they struggled to keep up with rally cars on the faster stretches. By the time Subaru began making a serious attempt to win the Safari, progress demanded a helicopter (carrying the pilot, the hazard spotter and a doctor) per rally car. Helicopters were sometimes imported on a temporary basis from South Africa and, naturally, they needed an element of servicing as well. The bill was frequently in the order of £50,000.

Back on the ground – and no matter which country they found themselves in that week – mechanics needed to be competent drivers and navigators, capable of foraging for themselves and doing without much sleep. They might not see many of the rest of the team, let alone the opposition, for days at a stretch. It was hard going, but already some way removed from the rules of engagement when Prodrive was formed, as the FIA imposed no distance limitations of any kind until the spate of serious Group B accidents in 1986. International rallying certainly wasn't an 'office hours' sport by the 1990s, as was sometimes claimed, but the mechanic had at least the prospect of a few hours in bed every night.

Preparing for each rally was a vastly more complicated exercise. Hotels, flights and ferry crossings were booked months in advance, much as they are now, but movements during the rally had to be planned in far more detail. The moment the organisers issued the route, either of Prodrive's service co-ordinators (John Kennard and Ken Rees in the mid-1990s) or perhaps one of the co-drivers, would set off with maps and roadbooks, combing the countryside for service points. They might be in farmyards or garages, or simply at the roadside. Permission to use the site might be necessary – a fee had to be paid in certain instances – and competition was fierce: decent locations, especially in remote, mountainous countryside, were hard to find.

If there happened to be a lay-by, the competition was at its most intense during the event, when 'first-come, first-served' applied, and leaving the hotel early might earn a winning advantage; it never quite led to blows. A site where a helicopter could land was often an asset.

Once the route had been inspected and the service points decided, maps had to be prepared for each service crew, with time schedules and diagrams of the service points. Some teams also supplied 'tulip', roadbook-style instructions. Prodrive rarely bothered: Spiller, then the Team Manager, maintained that his mechanics were resourceful enough to manage with a map.

Prodrive used Mercedes vans that were big enough to require tachographs and therefore

Service planning was an intricate operation. The page from a Prodrive Safari service schedule gives an idea of the required attention to detail.

prodrive

555 SAFARI RALLY 1996 DATE: 07 April PAGE: 3-3
LEG: Three FROM: Nairobi – Nakuru Rd TO: Seyabei

FEATURE	INTERVAL TOTAL	REMARKS	FEATURE	INTERVAL TOTAL	REMARKS
1	0·00 / 0·00	Same as 3-2/3	7 RALLY TC35	9·14 / 81·06	'NTULELE' / PURKO HOTEL NTULELE / HARD TO SEE
2	0·27 / 0·27		8	0·42 / 81·48	
3	19·77 / 20·04	KENYA PIPELINE CO. LTD PUMPING STATION 22	9 SA TC36 RALLY	9·46 / 90·94	SERVICE AREA 36b / 'IL DAMAT' / OFFICAL ROADBOOK PAGE 156/03
4 RALLY	29·28 / 49·32	'SUSWA' / NGONG 67km E418 / OFFICIAL ROADBOOK PAGE 170/08	10 SA	7·44 / 98·38	SERVICE AREA 37a / 'KERRERIE'
5 SA	3·08 / 52·40	SERVICE AREA 38b / 'SUSWA'	11 FROM TC RALLY	1·49 / 99·87	'SEYABEI' / OFFICIAL ROADBOOK PAGE 169/03
6	19·52 / 71·92	SPORTSMAN NAIREGI-ENKARE 5km / ROAD WORKS AND POTHOLES NEXT 28km	12		

555 SUBARU WORLD RALLY TEAM

added heavily to Spiller's workload. Few rallies' time schedules in any way tallied with a van driver's permitted hours. The result was a fiendishly complicated plan in which a chase car crew often drove the van to its first point, while the van crew drove the chase car, which didn't require a tachograph. The crews would swap vehicles at the service point, then swap back later in the day when the van crew had run out of hours. It wasn't unknown for extra mechanics to be taken, purely to comply with the unbending requirements of the tachograph.

'We tried to plan beforehand how long it would take to get from A to B, but you couldn't predict that and you couldn't plan how long it would take to pack up a service point even. It wasn't computerised: it was done in your head on event,' Rees promised.

The resources ploughed into the operation varied from rally to rally and manufacturer to manufacturer. The nature of the route and a brisk time schedule made the Acropolis one of the most demanding events. It wasn't unknown for teams to bring up to 14 vans, each laden with thousands of pounds' worth of equipment. Spare gearboxes in each van might total over £400,000 between them, to say nothing of the other components. Prodrive thrived in this environment.

'We had 25 or 30 people and there wasn't much to choose between the best and the worst, and they were all bloody capable, so you didn't often find yourself at a disadvantage. That probably did give us an advantage, even against some of the factory teams. They would have ten star guys and they probably had to bring ten out of the factory to make the numbers up.

'I think, for a long time, we did as well as anybody, because I think even sort of modestly putting it, we were very well organised, second only to Lancia's "Throw a massive resource at it". We were very good, for the size of team that we were, at doing the job then. We went through a spell of not

Although plenty of Prodrive staff could have found their way round mid-Wales blindfolded, more familiar ground (the 1997 RAC Rally in this case) also required detailed planning.

Schedule - Leg 2, Monday 24 November

SS No	Name	Time of Day	Comp Dist Km.	% Comp Complete	Serv Area	Serv Type	Time of Day	Serv Time	S3	S4	T	Tk	A	B	C	D	E	M	Dr	Mh1	Mh2	Per Car	3 Cars	S3	S4	Tk
	Hotel																									
	Restart, Cheltenham	5:00																	Dr							
	Hereford (E)				E	Serv	6:16	0:10	S3				A	B	C	D	E	M			Mh2	[28]				
12	Radnor	7:25	18.65	20																						
	Builth Wells (F)				F	Serv	8:25	0:20				Tk	A	B	C	D	E	M	Dr		Mh2	49	147			147
13	Hafren	9:52	39.46	30																						
	Dolgellau (G)				G	Serv	11:39	0:20		S4	T		A	B	C	D	E	M	Dr	Mh1		50	150		150	
14	Pantperthog 1	12:32	15.40	34																						
15	Dyfi	13:02	23.88	40																						
16	Gartheiniog	13:37	14.95	44																						
	Regroup (10')	14:26																	Dr							
	Dolgellau (H)				H	Serv	14:41	0:20		S4	T		A	B	C	D	E	M	Dr	Mh1		55	165		165	
17	Sweet Lamb	16:06	29.05	52																						
18	Myherin	16:54	17.53	56																						
	Builth Wells (I)				I	Serv	18:19	0:45	S3			Tk	A	B	C	D	E	M	Dr	Mh1	Mh2	52	156			156
	Cheltenham P/F	21:16																								
	Restock at Builth Wells (I)								S3	S4	T	Tk	A	B	C	D	E									
	LEG TOTALS		158.92																				618	0	315	303

Radio Aircraft Schedule   6:00 Channel 1   8:50 Channel 2   9:30 Channel 1   15:00 Channel 2   15:40 Channel 1   19:15

Notes for Service.

Service 3 From Hereford go to Builth Wells to assist Truck. Keith Murray will take Sv. 3 unit that evening to Cardiff, Quality Hotel. D. Hartwell Etc. take car from Keith to Cardiff, leave keys at reception.

Service 4 From Restock go to hotel at Aberdare.

Truck Return to Cheltenham from restock.

Hereford Sv. Pt. E Refuel cars In Service.

Dolgellau Sv. Pt. G & H Refuel cars In Service.

making many mistakes, of not having duff bits or leaving bits behind. For a few years there, we were as good or better than anybody at pitching up in New Zealand, doing the job, being back home on a Tuesday and doing it again two weeks later,' Riddle maintained.

Prodrive knew how to have fun, too, but even professionals have the occasional lapse. On one occasion, when the cars were being collected from *parc ferme* after a rally, one of the mechanics indulged in a few doughnuts; the celebrations were abruptly terminated when the Impreza pirouetted into a hitherto-unnoticed skip.

However, the cost of unrestricted servicing and practising was excessive, and from the early 1990s onwards their reduction has been gradual, but remorseless. It started with limits on the length of pre-rally recces and the cars used; for this reason, there was never any need to use anything as highly tuned as an old Impreza rally car to practise, other

than on the Safari. Service restrictions first took the form of a ban on outside assistance between designated stages, then tightened as organisers were put under pressure to plan 'cloverleaf' routes: each day of the rally would loop around a central point and servicing was permitted nowhere else.

Devising and printing a service schedule ceased to be a combination of military exercise and desktop publishing. As Spiller explained, looking ahead to new regulations and shorter rallies in 1997: 'If you have standardisation on identifying service points and that's marked on the map, we no longer need to do our own maps – and that takes a day, to mark your maps and get them printed. I think you've also got to review the past. We produce things like the service schedule, because we've always done it. Well, a service schedule coped with 70 individual points, where people were up farm tracks. Now that we're going to five points a day and they're all common, and all the

When a World Championship has been won, no one gets overlooked in the celebrations. The team line up with Richard Burns and Robert Reid in Cardiff in November 2001.

information is common, basically the organisers can give us that and we don't need a service schedule any more. The information that we need to put on a service schedule can be printed on two sides of A4, whereas before it was a 40-page document, and that did take a bit of putting together.

'Averaging out, we're taking two service units plus our "mother" truck. Then we take dedicated mechanics for each of the competitors in a car each; then we have an

Subaru wouldn't be complete without Ken Rees. Assistant Team Manager in 2004, he has been involved with the team since 1990.

engineering car with all the specialists, we have a management car, then we have a "gash" car that looks after all the routine jobs, like refuelling, tyres, windscreens and any spillover, really.

'What we're doing now is far more regimented. Instead of just hauling a team together and saying, "Right, we need a team manager, a co-ordinator, a Colin McRae engineer, a Kenneth Eriksson engineer, we need a number one [mechanic] for each car plus three mechanics, we need an engine engineer, an electrician, transmission [specialist]," and then basically you say, "Who in the team can fulfil those roles?", we're actually doing a fairly involved computer programme, whereby you can select the team. You fire up 'electrician' and it gives you four names who are available, have the right jabs, the right uniform, what have you, click a button and he's on his way to Argentina.

'There's far less dithering about and individually getting up a party to do an event. I think it's actually quite a good thing, because it's making us think and become far more disciplined.'

Spiller was planning for a comparatively wide-ranging rally. By 2002 there was scarcely a World Championship round that used more than one service point throughout, and the provision for emergency service points granted in 2004 was on nothing like the old scale, because just two mechanics were permitted to work on each car and they were allowed to carry tools, but not spares.

Rees doesn't warm to the change. Now the Assistant Team Manager, the first rally he watched was the 1966 Welsh. He can remember the number plate of the winning Cortina and reminisces fondly about watching RAC Rallies and Gulf Londons, about driving and navigating Avengers in the 1970s and '80s. A 'cloverleaf' route around a central hub, no matter how sensible and sociable, will never enthuse someone brought up with the thrill of the chase, of moving from point to point, rarely stationary for more than half hour. Like Wilson, he can understand the reasons, though, and points out that change has created a different set of priorities.

'Whereas you planned an emergency, or at most a ten-minute, service park years ago, now we plan for four days or five days on site with all the equipment and everything to be self-sufficient for that time. It's different, it's totally different. It's easier, because every organiser has a service park co-ordinator and you're dealing with one man, who knows what you want, but the challenge isn't so great as it was years ago, when you'd go out for that five- or six- or seven-day recce and you'd come back and do your paperwork, and do your own maps and everything. The job has changed a lot now: you don't need the maps to get people around. They only have to have hotel-to-service-park, service-park-to-hotel, so that side of it has gone.

'But the other side of it is because it's a big hospitality show now, you've got to make sure your vehicles are tidy. You've always got to look nice all the time. The media are always watching you, the VIPs, so you're always under the eye of sponsors and world media. It's more of keeping your service park a lot tidier now and more efficient.

'It's a changed sport now, isn't it? We all work within a huge area for four days together. Before, you would rarely see other people. Now, we hold meetings on site, we do planning on site, we run it as an office. So the appeal is there for the job satisfaction side, to make sure 40 people come here, they work well, they go home happy and we go home hopefully with a result, and that everything on our side works,' he explained.

The planning remains an intricate process. It begins in earnest the moment the calendar is finalised. Hotels are booked, flights investigated at the very least. Rees reckons on spending eight days in the host country for a European round of the World Championship and up to 12 for a non-European rally, which may involve booking a local workshop. New rallies generally require an extra trip in advance, purely to get the lie of the land. Freight has become Keith Murray's responsibility and is sent increasingly by air as more rallies join the

World Championship and the need to move large numbers of cars and spares declines.

As recently as the 1998 Rally of New Zealand, Prodrive deployed 21 vehicles, including three rally cars. Eight of the assorted lorries and cars were hired locally. In the 21st century, there might be three large trucks (Rees would reckon on bringing a total length of 130 lay metres of vehicles to a rally in Europe), but because the mechanics are going to a central point, a couple of minibuses will generally suffice to take them to and from the hotel.

'In 1995, say, we would have taken a lot more smaller vehicles. We would take more in parts then, but we would take less in equipment such as terracing, flooring – what we call the show equipment, everything that goes with the hospitality side,' Rees said, providing a snapshot of planning for early 2004. 'To Mexico, for instance, we didn't take any vehicles, because it's an indoor service park and one service park the whole event. Anything we want we hire locally just for the short time we're there, so we fly eight

Tyre cutting is a means of fine-tuning a tread pattern, but it is rarely a leisurely process, especially on Tarmac rallies, when minor changes in the weather can make a world of difference.

ton of equipment out there, plus rally cars.

'All that goes by ship is the reconnaissance cars, because everything else, spares will be flown, tool boxes will be flown, the terracing and the easy-ups, etc. will all be flown, because it's wanted for New Zealand and we can't ship it from Mexico to New Zealand. We have scaled down now to having one set of kit which will do 16 events, so we have to fly it, but it does save having two lots of kit, as we've had in the past – a long-haul kit and a short-haul kit. But when the long-haul events before this year went down to be only four events, it was silly having millions of pounds of stuff tied up just for four events.'

It remains an expensive business. In 2004, Prodrive budgeted to spend over £1,500,000 on transport alone.

Staying awake has taken on a new significance. There isn't a great deal a mechanic has to do for most of a sprint race, if anything, but at least the cars come past the pits at frequent intervals. On a contemporary rally, hours drag between service intervals and the cars could easily be 50 miles off. Mechanics read or might watch the previous day's or rally's action, which is likely to be displayed on a video screen somewhere in the service area; and they have taken to bringing laptops for their own amusement. Prodrive has also formed a partnership with a firm of management consultants, Performance First, and in 2002, they started devising games for small teams to attempt between service points, a development of training courses between rallies.

'It's been good for the team, because it builds a team within a team. Some take a lot of interest in the stages when they're happening, they come and see the stage times coming in, some will just go away. There are always little jobs to do after service, tidying up, but we're working at keeping everyone happy and keeping them busy,' Rees said.

Yet, while new rules have appreciably changed the job itself, they have made surprisingly little difference to the number of people taken to most rallies. When Moore started, he was the deputy rally engineer

reporting to Lapworth. In 1995 Prodrive hired additional engineers for each driver, much like a Grand Prix team. Simon Cole acted as McRae's and then Burns's engineer, while Genon worked with Piero Liatti. Moore (who transferred to the customer division for a year) was brought back to act as Kankkunen's engineer in 1999 and 2000, and Genon has since become Solberg's engineer. Michael Zetos was recruited from Ralliart to liaise firstly with Mäkinen, then with Hirvonen.

As the cars have become more sophisticated, engine and data experts have also become necessary. STi sends an engineer as well. Since the end of 2003 the number of mechanics has declined, and one data engineer has been taken to each rally rather than two, but there are more catering staff and a physiotherapist as well as a doctor. Spiller estimated that the team would consist of around 38 people per rally in 1997. Following the ban on gravel note crews, Rees reckoned on a drop to 40 per European rally in 2004, reduced to 36 on other continents. He added that a handful of extra people would be brought periodically to report on weather conditions, notably on Tarmac rallies, where their contribution to choosing tyres is vital.

All told, Prodrive employed around 75 staff as full-time members of the Subaru World Rally Team by 2004, but they are backed up by another 110 people within the organisation, who work in other fields, too, but provide essential engineering support. In addition, STi has an 11-strong team with a WR Car in Japan, headed by Shigeo Sugaya, concentrating on engines and durability.

Over time, the use of individual staff has become more systematic. Any team is at the mercy of the calendar, and in 2003 some Subaru personnel were away for 40–45 days at a stretch towards the end of the season, but the aim is to rotate them as the number of rallies increases, so that only a handful attend all events.

'We don't do more than nine or ten with certain people. You've got to make sure they don't get too exhausted towards the end of the year. It can pull you down a bit,' Rees explained.

It has always been the case that the man who's best with a sledgehammer in a crisis isn't necessarily the best car builder. Over time, procedures have been refined and preparation standards have been raised. There are almost invariably seven or eight mechanics at Banbury preparing cars for the next rally, to a schedule planned as carefully as that for the events themselves. In 2003 Prodrive constructed 12 works Imprezas. For 2004 the target was ten, but as Riddle emphasised, 'car' is a term to be used advisedly.

'A car is only a car for a long weekend about three times a year. We'll use far more shells than we will cars, as it were,' he said.

Figures need to be considered in that light, but the number of cars built is substantial nonetheless. Solberg's 2004 Rally of New Zealand car was the 105th World Rally Car to be constructed by Subaru.

The building and stocking of components is just as carefully planned, and confirms co-drivers' worst suspicions: lengthily compiled figures show that the door most frequently damaged in an accident is the right rear, followed by the right front, the left rear and the left front – which is very rarely damaged. Similarly, the right-hand suspension is far more likely to be damaged than the left. All works Imprezas are left-hand drive.

Many people stay. From the outset, David Richards had a policy of offering a career, not a job.

'I've always got this notion that if you can bring someone on in your own organisation then it is far more worthwhile,' he said. 'It binds people together. If you always recruit from the outside when you've got a vacancy that appears to be a big opportunity, or a senior vacancy, people inside get really annoyed about it and you actually de-motivate people. If you take people in at the bottom and you prove that you've got an organisation that develops people right the way through to the top level, it motivates everybody involved and pulls them together.'

Riddle is a case in point. One of the

original seven, he switched to co-ordinating freight in the mid-1990s, and rarely appeared on any rally other than the Safari, when a famously placid temperament helped make him the perfect hazard spotter from a helicopter. He has since become Planning and Purchasing Manager, which involved a good deal of liaison with STi on the supply of certain parts, but little other daily involvement with the World Championship team. The new priority became strengthening Subaru's involvement in Group N.

Alan McGuinness was McRae's chief mechanic for a time, then moved on to managing the recce team, then to managing the US Championship programme. When that was curtailed, he showed immediate flair as part of the sales team.

Thus, staying with the organisation isn't at all the same as remaining closely involved with the World Championship team. Pursuing the world title is a demanding,

John Spiller (left) and David Lapworth were key members of Prodrive practically from its inception. They were old hands by the time the Subaru deal was done.

time-consuming job, still anti-social in many ways. Age, marriage and children can militate against remaining a mechanic, or certainly against being a travelling mechanic. Those who do like it sometimes relish the variety above all.

'There's boys who come in the game and they do five years and say, "Right, that's it, there's something else to do in life." We've had boys working in this team who've done every formula. Some people say they want to do Formula 1, Grand Prix bike, Superbike, and they work their way round,' Howarth said.

But the changing nature of the job has also changed the type of people involved. It's inevitable that the older hands regard tearing round the countryside as the good old days. They never sound dismissive about their successors, but they don't enthuse about the task they're set. They argue, too, that the evolution of the Impreza has also created a different sort of mechanic.

Riddle put it fairly, acknowledging that a transition has taken place, without denigrating the men in the workshop.

'You very quickly lose the sort of people that you give a map and a van and say, "Go there and deal with whatever happens. We may come and help you." It wasn't just here. It was in every team. There was a certain type of guy who could do that job,' he said. He suggested that such people may now be attracted to cross-country rallies or sports car racing.

'I think now it's much more attention to detail – fastidious almost,' he added. 'And nearly an acknowledgement, Formula 1-wise, "I do my bit and if my bit's bolted on and it's right and it works, that's fine." There's not so much all-round stuff now. In the early days, everybody would deal with every problem and that was the way it was. Then you start taking your engine man, and you start taking your electrician, and you start taking your damper man, and gradually you sort of foster this situation where, "You'd better not touch that unless the engine man is there," which is completely a Formula 1-created situation. I would say the guys

downstairs have got to be attentive, methodical and thorough.'

'Every now and again, I've been doing tyres, I can sit back and watch, and then you can say, "That was pretty impressive, that. That was good." But it's not so broad-based. I mean, you might have done six or seven services a day, whereas now you're only doing three or four and you might end up with nothing much to do on three of them, so it's more difficult to say, "He's good, he's really good," because they don't get the chance to shine that they used to. That's not to say that they're not good,' Wilson commented.

The growing sophistication of the cars is the main cause of greater specialisation.

'I can vividly recall an Acropolis when we rebuilt 94 struts one night on the car park halfway up the hill to Delphi. You had a strut body, an insert that probably came from Bilstein at the time, a spring, two platforms and some grease. Four of us rebuilt 94 of them one night, no problem at all. Latterly, when we were doing our own, before the Sachs deal, we had a staff of six whose whole job was building and rating shock absorbers, and with all the changes to the service that had happened, we were probably only taking 10 or 12 sets to a rally. That's the way all of it has gone' Riddle said.

Simon Baker joined as an apprentice from college in Banbury in 1994, and finally went on a rally (after 18 months of learning the trade, sweeping floors and building cars for the test team) in Catalonia in 1995; it was some place to start. He's heard all the tales, but didn't see much of roadside servicing himself. Nevertheless, he pointed out that no one would do the job if they didn't find it stimulating. Rather than listen for a misfire, his role as one of the cornermen – one of five mechanics per car – is very often to follow instructions issued from the number one mechanic, who relies on instructions from the engineers after they've spoken to the driver and studied the data logger; that's the theory, anyway. To that extent, advancing technology may have limited his responsibilities, but it hasn't made his job less difficult.

'The technology on the cars now is unbelievable. We've had like a few instances sometimes where we've changed every mechanical part on the car, because there's a misfire, and then it turns out to be a little glitch in the software. It's sometimes the last thing to be looked at rather than the first thing. Normally you have like two to three weeks to build them and if you've got all the bits there, two people, it's steady away. You don't have to work too many late nights, which is good,' he said.

The worst job on an Impreza is replacing the turbocharger boost pack, because it is hidden at the back of the engine bay and therefore much of the job has to be done blind. Shorter rallies mean less time away from home, but it remains a high-pressure means of earning a living, in which major repairs are still performed against the clock. Wilson recalls McRae's Malaysian escape, Howarth thinks of a similar incident involving Bertie Fisher on a Circuit of Ireland, when a gatepost became a Legacy front panel for the rest of the rally. Baker remembers the unlikely recreation of Solberg's Impreza after

his Corsican shakedown smash in 2003, with more time available, but a daunting task to be done. As he points out, centralised service gives no second chances: there is no tightening up any suspect or forgotten bolts ten miles down the road.

Some teams – BMC's Mini squad at Abingdon for instance – were locally recruited. Their spirit and character have been in part derived from geography. Prodrive doesn't fall into that category. Baker is a Londoner brought up in Chipping Norton and might be regarded as local by adoption, but Howarth came from Clitheroe, McGuinness from the Wirral, Rees from Cardiff, Riddle from Bristol and Wilson (who swore for years that he would never move south before settling in Oxfordshire) from Huddersfield. That's merely the British side of the team. Prodrive's international reputation has drawn people from the corners of the globe. The Midlands have become home to an expatriate community, all fired by the same thirst for competition, quietly settled in the pretty Cotswold villages and market towns that are in part the

By the 21st century, the roles were reversed. The service crews took up position for the week and the rally cars returned to the hub – Lamia on the 2003 Acropolis in this case – at regulation intervals.

dormitories of the British motorsport industry.

Genon and Loriaux have been cases in point, both Belgian, both graduates of domestic universities and Cranfield, both long-term employees at Prodrive. Genon comes from Huy in southern Belgium, like François Duval's co-driver, Stéphane Prevot, and joined Prodrive in 1997 after a year with AP Racing. He seemed surprised to be asked how he found life abroad.

'I'm fairly integrated. In our case, we're quite mixed in. You'd have to after that long time,' he answered. He noted that a small Franco-Belgian community had settled in Leamington Spa, bolstered by an influx of French engineers at Mitsubishi, but they don't form a tribe of their own.

From the beginning of their relationship, Prodrive has had a hand in the marketing and promoting of Subaru. Prodrive negotiated the sponsorship deal with BAT

and Prodrive brought in Stevens. Winning rallies is a blend of engineering and teamwork, but the investment is justified as a promotional exercise. Subaru's use of the rallying has been an object lesson in transforming its image, to the extent that it generated Martin Beck-Burridge's academic study, *Building Brand, Business and Profit: The Story of Subaru and Motorsport*. The long-term partnership has thrived thanks to men such as Ian Parry and Colin Clark, not simply to Lapworth and Farley. Indeed, the attention devoted to building and maintaining the image may be said to have strengthened and prolonged the relationship between the two companies, and encouraged Subaru to attach so much value to the sport itself.

BAT was a significant factor, particularly in the Far East in the 1990s. It used to exasperate the drivers that they had to attend an endless round of PR functions, especially

First the engineer, now the boss, David Lapworth is a pragmatist with a gift for communication. He formed a close working relationship with Petter Solberg.

when rivals in other teams were left to their own devices, but cigarette companies have generally set the lead in promotion, and while McRae in particular treated it with all the enthusiasm of a trip to the dentist, Subaru undeniably benefited.

Riddle isn't sure that there is, or perhaps ever was, such a thing as a 'Prodrive person'. Like some of his older comrades, he suspects that the raw enthusiasm that used to fuel the team has been unavoidably diluted by its growing size. When 200 people are involved, it inevitably becomes an industrial exercise, a cog in the motor industry as much as a team.

Yet it continues to attract people like Solberg's chief mechanic, John McLean. An Ulsterman, he used to cycle to Willie McVicker's workshop near Belfast after school and watch until he finally pestered McVicker into giving him a job. He's run his own team and also worked for Ralliart, leaving Prodrive once after a disagreement with Howarth. He's old enough to remember a time when he couldn't turn to an electrician to diagnose a misfire and when, back in Ireland, any mechanic would help an 'opposing' driver, because everyone wanted to win fair and square, not on mere reliability. His dedication to Solberg has bordered on devotion and his sheer zest for competition leaves a powerful impression.

In any case, there is a footloose contingent who would regard taking the same route to work month in, month out as a form of imprisonment: Howarth frequently attended 35 rallies a year. Rees hasn't missed a World Championship rally the team has contested since 1992 and was a regular member of the Asia-Pacific squad as well.

Some stay in hotels in the evenings and hoard day money. Wilson would always prefer to go out and spend it in a restaurant. The travelling is sometimes a chore, but often part of the appeal. Rees reckons on spending 13 days a year in aircraft.

'It's a large slice out of your life. I spend more time on aeroplanes than people have holidays in total sometimes,' he observed.

Subaru and Prodrive have been confronted by a new challenge in the 21st century, pre-

eminently from the French manufacturers, Peugeot and Citroën. Howarth doesn't accept that his opponents' size makes them invincible.

'I think the underdog side of the team is very strong. Everyone will give 100% and it's not insurmountable, beating them. We showed that we can beat them,' he said.

He accepts that a momentary lapse from the driver can ruin everything, but stresses that this is in the nature of the sport.

'I think you've got to be a bit open-minded about it. Anybody in the team can ruin everything – anybody. If somebody's not doing the job right, not paying enough attention to detail – anything from turning up late, because it has a knock-on effect on the team. But there should be no person that you hinge all of it on. Everyone should take the same amount of responsibility. If everybody takes the same amount of responsibility, you will get what you're looking for. The team is a major factor, for sure, but the key factor is the bloke behind the wheel.'

The lulls between service intervals are often lengthy, but once the car arrives, the pace is furious. In Cyprus in 2003, the crew's efforts were abundantly rewarded.

8 Perpetuating success

It would be wrong to have described the Asia-Pacific Rally Championship as a sleepy backwater, but when Subaru signed its first contract with British American Tobacco late in 1992, it would be fair to say that there was a gulf between it and the World Championship, as there was to all of the FIA's regional championships. Thanks in large part to Subaru and BAT, it was closed with dizzying speed.

Subaru's Asia-Pacific campaign was conceived primarily because the Far East and, above all, China were the biggest markets for 555 cigarettes. Yet, although the programme was first and foremost a promotional exercise for BAT, it could never be dismissed as a sponsor-pleasing exercise; it demanded far too much in the way of resources for that. Vast distances between most of the rallies made planning just as intricate an operation as the World Championship itself, and in any case the two overlapped, because Australia's and New Zealand's World Championship rallies also qualified for Asia-Pacific points in the 1990s. The same service vehicles and rally cars were very often used for both.

But there was an additional, daunting requirement attached to the Asia-Pacific series: the Hong Kong–Peking Rally. Its geographical sweep carried an echo of the sport's past, of classic, long-dead, long-distance rallies such as the Alpine or the Liège. It became an anachronism within months of first being held in 1985, as the FIA imposed stage distance limitations in 1986. It didn't sit easily with contemporary rallies when it was revived in the 1990s (it was

shelved for a number of years following the Tiananmen Square massacre) because there was simply no need for the start and finish to be so far removed in view of the permitted stage distance: Hong Kong–Wuhan – the approximate halfway point – would have been more like it. But it was still an epic, an adventure as much as a rally, and it posed a challenge like no other event in the region. The fact that it was sponsored by 555 redoubled its importance to Prodrive.

Even Hong Kong, for all its commercial bustle, didn't offer much in the way of facilities, the mechanics grumbling darkly that you'd struggle to do anything more complicated than change a windscreen. As an engineering base, they reckoned it was no substitute for Kuala Lumpur or Bangkok. It was nevertheless lavishly equipped compared to what lay across the border.

'It was logistically horrendous, but that was a really good challenge. We'd go on a 12-day recce and come back a fortnight later and do the event. You'd leave Hong Kong, you'd be into China, a seven-day event across there, 4,500 kilometres, with 16 vehicles plus three rally cars. You'd just keep your fingers crossed that everybody got across, because you'd go days without seeing them or talking to them,' Rees commented. He loved it.

The Prodrive men took it in their stride, by and large, and their cause was aided considerably by choosing Bourne to lead the team. A tough, capable driver, the New Zealander and the Legacy were in a class of their own in 1993 and he romped to another convincing championship success a year later in an Impreza 555, backed up by Burns, who

Subaru's men were old hands in the Far East by the time the China Rally replaced Hong Kong–Peking in 1997. Colin McRae cruised to an untroubled victory in his WRC97.

was in his first season outside Britain. The Imprezas were first and second in Malaysia as well as on the Hong Kong–Peking.

But the stakes were raised appreciably when Mitsubishi joined the fray, attracted by the chance to gain publicity in burgeoning Far Eastern markets. The Lancer Evo IIIs were generally a match for the Imprezas, especially when the cars were run by the British-based World Championship team, and Mitsubishi had no hesitation in using its works drivers, Eriksson and Mäkinen. The former adapted well to sweltering heat and slimy plantation tracks, depriving Bourne and Subaru of the 1995 title.

This was a sideshow, but in no sense an afterthought. The latest works cars were used, and the drivers demanded gravel note crews to check stages for last-minute hazards. It had become a World Championship in miniature.

Prodrive could ill afford to lose. It deftly undermined Mitsubishi by poaching Eriksson for 1996 and occasionally sent McRae, too. He led a Subaru one–two–three on the

opening round in Thailand, supported by Eriksson and Liatti, but the Swede was the linchpin of the campaign and he did Subaru proud. The season concluded embarrassingly, every works Impreza crashing out of the last Hong Kong–Peking before the halfway point, thereby allowing Mitsubishi to retain the manufacturers' trophy, but Eriksson had fulfilled his role and retained the drivers' championship.

Most top drivers had come to dislike the series by then. The professionalism and commitment of the works teams imposed severe strains on organisers who were generally amateur and sometimes struggled to keep stages closed to other traffic. It was perhaps no bad thing that expanding the World Championship and demanding that the manufacturers tackled it in its entirety curtailed their Asia-Pacific involvement in 1997, although Subaru dutifully contested and won the first two China Rallies, both of them backed by 555.

Bourne hadn't quite finished with the Asia-Pacific series, though, winning it for a third

Serving the sponsor bulked large in Subaru's priorities in China. Richard Burns (left) and Juha Kankkunen pose dutifully in front of a suitable background.

time in 2000 with his own team and Caltex sponsorship. It's an indication of the commitment required that he had to use two cars, relying on his Impreza WR Car for the Australasian rallies, but building a new Impreza 555 for the northern events. His judgement was flawless: the Group A car was rugged and reliable and, in his hands, more than equal to the opposition.

Bourne persisted with Group A into 2002, building an Impreza 44S to the old regulations and winning the Hokkaido Rally – the forerunner to the Rally of Japan. He reckoned that it was a sensible compromise between cost and performance, but its future was cut short when anything more potent than a Group N car was banned from the Asia-Pacific series.

Any serious privateer resorting to a Group A car in any part of the globe was bound to raise an eyebrow by that stage. WR Cars were inevitably a more expensive and awkward proposition for the non-factory driver because they were, by and large, hand-built prototypes: even for a car such as the Impreza, which had much in common with its showroom counterpart, there was no prospect of buying a written-off road car, a new bodyshell and some spares, then preparing a rally car at home. Every private Impreza WR Car is ex-works.

It did little to dampen the demand. From 1997–2000 Prodrive sold 52 Impreza WR Cars and its customer division, headed by Richard Taylor, swelled to the extent that it employed 70 staff and turned over £12,000,000 in 2000. It had nine engine builders at Banbury, independent of the works team and booked for four months in advance, and five account managers handling a portion of the globe each. Prodrive-tended Imprezas competed everywhere from Australia to Indonesia and the United States.

This was a tribute to the excellence of the car and the team. As a relatively small manufacturer, Subaru's importers were rarely in a position to fund national championship programmes – not when a second-hand WRC99 cost £225,000 and Prodrive parted with P2000s for £295,000. Accordingly,

Subaru privateers wanted what they perceived as a winning car.

From an early stage, cars were sold to customer teams, notably Ken McKinstry in Northern Ireland, ART in Italy and Cilti Sport in France. Later, Italian teams such as Procar bought plenty of cars; for a time, half of all ex-works Imprezas went to Italy. However, Prodrive had run cars on behalf of customers itself since its BMW days and the policy was extended and refined when it switched to Subaru.

Krzysztof Holowczyc and Andrea Navarra became European Rally Champions in 1997 and 1998 in Prodrive-assisted Imprezas, and the incentive to run privateers on something not far removed from a factory footing increased still further in 1998 when the FIA introduced the Teams Cup. It was essentially a prize for privateers using WR Cars in the World Championship, and Prodrive became involved in running drivers such as Freddy Dor (a long-standing customer who had also rallied its M3s) the double World Group N Champion, Grégoire de Mevius, and the

'Possum' Bourne (pictured in his WRC98 on the 2001 Rally of New Zealand) played a central part in Subaru's growing stature in rallying. No one drove a wider range of Subaru rally cars.

Much the best Japanese driver to have driven a works Subaru, Toshihiro Arai was a prolific winner in the Teams Cup and latterly in the Production World Championship.

Oman driver, Hamed Al Wahaibi, as the Prodrive Allstars. The investment justified recruiting an engineer, Graham Moore, and in time David Campion (not the sales manager, but one of the key figures in the sales division) promised that he could offer a range of facilities, from test drivers to doctors, physiotherapists and gravel note crews. By 2000, customer activities justified seven engineers. This was an expensive, but high-quality service: the test drivers included Thiry, who had been a works driver in 1998, and Simon Jean-Joseph, who was runner-up in the French Championship that year in a Cilti Sport Impreza 555 and later joined the factory team on an occasional basis.

The testing process was geared to driver preference, but Allstars staff tactfully acknowledged that it was also adapted to the needs of privateers. A World Championship contender drives with unflinching commitment; given anything less, a WR Car becomes horribly unforgiving. Setting a car up for all but the most gifted customers therefore involved subtle alterations to

suspension and transmission to make it easier to drive.

Campion's facilities even extended to honing the driver.

'Fitness, diet, training, physio, addressing physiological problems, eyesight, you name it, we will cover anything and everything, if it's necessary. But, again, it has a cost attached to it unfortunately. The general perception is that, yes, you have to be fit to drive rally cars, but probably not that fit. I'll be quite happy to say that I was one who wasn't necessarily "convinced". It seemed like a good thing to do, but I wasn't necessarily convinced that the depth that we seemed to be prepared to go to was absolutely necessary. But I've seen the proof of it now and I am 100% convinced,' he said in 2000.

In 1999 the Spaniard, Luis Climent, won the Teams Cup in an Impreza, and the following year Arai demolished his opponents in a Prodrive-run WRC99 entered under the Spike Subaru banner. In the process, he finished fourth overall on the Acropolis and sixth on the Safari, results of which many works drivers would have been proud. Campion suggested that some of his success could be attributed to the fitness programme – and observed that a fit, alert driver who does less damage to the car would consider the time and money spent on his own preparation well worthwhile.

By then, Prodrive was preparing to equip customer cars with the latest semi-automatic gearbox, but only if they were tended at Banbury, as it didn't want the technology falling into the wrong hands. WR Cars were getting to the stage where they were becoming difficult to run without factory help regardless of any conditions imposed when sold. Experienced mechanics took on a 1999 car with a degree of reluctance – they are honest enough to admit that they don't fully understand how they work – and subsequent models have become still more complicated. Like any rally car, a WR Car needs to be able to start from cold unaided in *parc ferme* on a sub-zero morning, but an engineer with a laptop is essential to guarantee that it runs satisfactorily;

electronics have all but dispelled the fond fantasy that a plucky privateer can sometimes take on the factories.

All those facilities are still available from Prodrive. In the meantime, increasing sophistication had raised the cost of a customer-tune WR Car, with a non-works, sequential, semi-automatic gearbox, to £330,000 by early 2004. But these were the dizzy peaks of amateur or semi-professional endeavour. The demise of the Teams Cup at the end of 2001 undermined the demand for Allstars, while the growing cost of WR Cars has led to their elimination from a growing number of regional and national championships, including both the Asia-Pacific and European series, as well as the Italian, Portuguese and Spanish Championships.

WR Car sales therefore declined, with a projected maximum of 16 in 2004, but under Taylor's replacement, Jason Hill, sales of Group N cars rocketed, Prodrive alone planning to sell 40 in 2004. Turnover remained much the same. Group N was long a source of exasperation to Prodrive, but the category is not and never has been its preserve. Introduced in the same year as Group A, Group N was intended originally as a national category (hence the 'N') for barely modified cars along the lines of the old Group 1. It has evolved a long way from that original, somewhat fuzzy vision, but it remains the most production-based of the international rally categories. Far more extensive modifications are allowed than in 1982, including larger brakes and non-synchromesh gears, but it is still possible to build a rally car from a standard car. While Prodrive would charge around £85,000 for a fully prepared Impreza to its highest Group N specification (an N10 car in company terms) in 2004, Subaru agents would sell a basic Impreza in unprepared form to rally drivers for   33,000, or about £23,000, depending on the exchange rate.

In its early years, the Impreza's successes in Group N form were isolated. Privateers reckoned that the Lancer was the superior car, and the practical support offered by Mitsubishi's Ralliart network in a range of

countries made an appreciable difference. Perhaps the back-up was the key factor, for Subaru succeeded where a range of other manufacturers had failed in conquering the Safari with Group N cars – surely the ultimate proof of mechanical resilience. The cars were prepared by Koseki's Subaru Motor Sports Group and, with the local hero, Patrick Njiru, on the team, they were not only capable of getting in the top five on occasion, but hogging a substantial share of the local headlines too.

But, as power outputs climbed, the Impreza's five-speed gearbox frequently buckled under the strain, for although a mandatory 32mm turbo restrictor limited power to around 280bhp, the flat-four still gave quite enough torque to wreck a gearbox originally designed for a 1300 car. When Trevor Cathers and Willie John Dolan became the first drivers to bring Imprezas to Ireland, on the Galway Rally, gearbox problems soon put a spanner in the works.

Subaru was not alone in this respect and salvation arrived in the form of a new rule

The original Subaru driver, 'Possum' Bourne drove Subarus everywhere from his native New Zealand to Argentina and Japan. His thriving team, based in Australia, has become part of his legacy.

Few drivers have rallied as wide a range of cars as the evergreen Stig Blomqvist. At the ripe old age of 56, he was still capable of winning the Production class at World Championship level in 2003, driving a Sutton-built Impreza.

No one could match Martin Rowe's blend of speed and consistency in 2003 and by the Rally Australia, the Manxman was able to pace himself to make sure of the Production world title.

permitting non-standard gears and non-standard gear engagement, provided the original ratios were retained. Prodrive developed a dog-engagement gear set that cured the problem – although it needed a little refinement when introduced in 2000 – and when the 44S was launched, it had a six-speed gearbox that was as good as indestructible.

It's an indication of the keenness of the rivalry with Mitsubishi that the last of the two-door Imprezas, known as GC8s, discarded the viscous coupling centre differential in favour of a programmable electro-magnetic type. Within two years, Prodrive staff reckoned that a Group N Impreza was as quick as a Group A car had been when it was introduced in 1994. By 2004, development and demand had led to the homologation of no fewer than six different gearboxes, made in Australia, Belgium, Britain, Italy and Japan.

Yet, despite David Higgins's efforts (which included Group N victory on the 2001 Rally GB) and some impressive performances from Arai, it took a concerted effort on Prodrive's part to demonstrate that the Impreza was truly a match for the Lancer. For 2002,

whole-hearted support was given to Arai and David Sutton's team, which ran the 1998 British Champion, Martin Rowe, and Stig Blomqvist. Arai was a regular winner, taking the class in New Zealand, Argentina and Cyprus, but Rowe's consistency was unmatched and a class victory in Australia helped make him a convincing Production World Champion. The tide had turned.

Prodrive hasn't made a habit of running Group N cars itself, but it became involved in Group N and in a mutant offshoot in the United States. Rallying in the US had not attracted much international attention since the Olympus Rally was dropped from the World Championship for 1989, but that changed rapidly when the US importer teamed up with Prodrive. A two-car assault was planned, spearheaded by Mark Lovell, the 1986 British Open Champion, with Ramana Lagemann in a Group N car. The programme was pieced together in a matter of weeks, yet Lovell crushed all opposition in 2001, starting the season in a World Rally Car.

This didn't quite accord with the spirit of Sports Car Club of America rules for the Pro-Rally series and Prodrive therefore developed

a hybrid Group N car for 2002. The SCCA permitted a 40mm intake restrictor that gave around 400bhp with a 'bastardised' Group A engine. Bigger brakes were fitted, but most of the running gear was Group N and, while the six-speed gearbox coped without protest, the differentials tended to wilt badly.

'This little centre differential when it's working is a brilliant piece of kit, but 400 horsepower and God knows how many Newton/metres of torque later used to shake it and all the bits used to fall out. It used to be like an overcooked bag of crisps,' a member of the team recalled.

'Perhaps what we should have done was run the centre differential locked, but we persevered. When the car was working, it was a beautiful car, it was untouchable. But as soon as one of the diffs started to go off, it upset the balance of the car and, from an engineering point of view, you ended up chasing your tail,' Campion reflected.

Subaru won the championship, anyway, through Higgins in an Impreza WRX, but Prodrive was convinced that its revised SCCA Impreza would fare much better in 2003. Lovell won the rally car class on the Pike's Peak Hillclimb in Colorado – a round of the rally championship – ending a run of three straight wins for Higgins and Mitsubishi, but it was the last event he finished. He crashed violently on the first stage of the Oregon Trail Rally in July and, along with his co-driver, Roger Freeman, he died at the scene. Pasi Hagstrom, one of the works team's test drivers, was drafted in and the Finn won the Wild West Rally, but the programme was wound up at the end of the season. Investment in an increasingly competitive championship and a unique type of lightly restricted engine had been heavy; Lovell's accident was hardly an encouragement.

By some margin, the most successful national championship programme has been in Australia and it owed a great deal to two men: Bourne, and the importer's General Manager, Nick Senior. As a New Zealander, Bourne had made occasional forays across the Tasman before and had won rounds of the Australian series in Legacys, finishing

third in 1993. Subaru Australia's unflagging support put the contest on an entirely different footing. Senior wanted rallying to play a central role in fostering Subaru's image, and in Bourne he found the perfect driver. Quite apart from his ability at the wheel, Bourne was promotable, determined and well connected. His links with STi and Prodrive did his chances no harm at all.

Bourne's main adversary was Neal Bates, who had been Australian Champion in Toyotas three years running when the Subaru driver arrived on the scene in 1996. Mitsubishi weighed in with Ed Ordynski and Group A Lancers, but Bourne was invariably a step ahead, and when WR Cars became available it was as though he had found another gear. He didn't always have the latest car – far from it, in fact – but it was always well prepared and he not only had good machinery but good tyres too. When he died in a strange and shocking accident, after his Forester was struck by another competitor when they were practising for the Race to the Sky Hillclimb in New Zealand in April 2003, he had been Australian Champion seven years running.

He had established a base in Sydney as well as his native Pukekohe, just south of Auckland, and at the time of his death he was adapting swiftly to new Australian rules that banned WR Cars and effectively turned it into a Group N championship. If his opponents imagined that this would change the outcome, they were to be disappointed. The 2003 Australian Champion was Cody Crocker, driving a Possum Bourne Motorsport Impreza. Commitment and professionalism were amply rewarded.

In Europe, Subaru's successes with privateers have been extensive yet unevenly and sometimes oddly distributed. Subaru drivers have thrived from Italy to Belgium, Germany to Russia, yet have also suffered somewhat from the vagaries of national championship regulations. By 2004, Stéphane Sarrazin had a good chance of becoming French Champion, thanks to a relaxation in national regulations, yet no Subaru driver became British Champion in the ten years following Burns's success in

1993, partly because restrictions on four-wheel-drive cars were a regular feature; this didn't prevent the likes of David Higgins, Tapio Laukkanen and Andrew Nesbitt from winning rallies outright. Higgins's 1999 results attracted the most attention, for the Manxman proved capable of embarrassing more powerful two-wheel-drive opposition in a Group N car run by Barretts, the Canterbury dealer. He followed it up with Group N victory on the Rally GB that year. It has taken a while, but the Impreza has started to gain a strong Group N following in Britain. The Welshman, Geoff Jones, was therefore given Prodrive support for 2004.

Across the Irish Sea, Nesbitt was in the vanguard of Subaru success. In Ireland, rally cars seem to conform to fashion: the Porsche age in the 1970s gave way to an Escort era, then to Chevettes, then to Escorts in Cosworth form and to Celicas, but the Impreza age has endured in the teeth of strong opposition. McKinstry and the late Bertie Fisher were the first to fly the flag. After years of near-misses, Fisher collected the first of four Circuit of Ireland wins in

Imprezas in 1995, and in 1996 he demolished all opposition in Ireland, taking the Circuit, the Ulster and his sixth victory on the Rally of the Lakes in Killarney.

Success fuelled success. Nesbitt, Derek McGarrity and Austin MacHale have been among those to have followed suit. It has become near-inevitable that Donegal, the Ulster and the Circuit of Ireland are won by Imprezas, and just as likely that they take the Tarmac rounds of the British Championship. Indeed, Irish rallying has thrived to such a degree that it has become the strongest market for Impreza WR Cars.

'WR Cars per capita, the highest ratio has got to be in Ireland,' Campion suggested.

Worldwide, STi intends to capitalise on its more recent triumphs in Group N, appointing Donaldson to establish a network of agents offering cars, spares and assistance across Europe, linked via the internet. One of those agents is none other than Mäkinen; it would be difficult to imagine a better source of advice for a young driver. Subaru's success in rallying will be not merely sustained, but perpetuated.

It was a sign of the Production World Championship's growing competitiveness that Alister McRae registered for the 2004 series. He was immediately one of the pacesetters in a RED-tuned Impreza.

Appendix
Works Impreza results

555 = Subaru Impreza 555
WRC97 = Subaru Impreza WRC97
WRC98 = Subaru Impreza WRC98
WRC99 = Subaru Impreza WRC99
WRC00 = Subaru Impreza WRC2000
WRC01 = Subaru Impreza WRC2001
WRC02 = Subaru Impreza WRC2002
WRC03 = Subaru Impreza WRC2003

1993

1000 Lakes Rally 27–29 August
A. Vatanen/B. Berglund   555   2nd
M. Alén/I. Kivimäki   555   Crashed

RAC Rally 21–24 November
A. Vatanen/B. Berglund   555   5th
C. McRae/D. Ringer   555   Rtd, overheating

1994

Monte Carlo Rally 22–27 January
C. Sainz/L. Moya   555   3rd
C. McRae/D. Ringer   555   10th

Rally of Portugal 1–4 March
C. Sainz/L. Moya   555   4th
C. McRae/D. Ringer   555   Rtd, fire

Tour of Corsica 5–7 May
C. Sainz/L. Moya   555   2nd
C. McRae/D. Ringer   555   Rtd, accident damage

Acropolis Rally 29–31 May
C. Sainz/L. Moya   555   1st
C. McRae/D. Ringer   555   Excluded

Rally of Indonesia 17–19 June
P. Bourne/T. Sircombe   555   2nd
R. Burns/R. Reid   555   Rtd

Rally of Argentina 30 June–2 July
C. Sainz/L. Moya   555   2nd
C. McRae/D. Ringer   555   Rtd, accident damage

Rally of New Zealand 29–31 July
C. McRae/D. Ringer   555   1st
C. Sainz/L. Moya   555   Rtd, engine
P. Bourne/T. Sircombe   555   Crashed

Rally of Malaysia 13–15 August
P. Bourne/T. Sircombe   555   1st
R. Burns/R. Reid   555   2nd

1000 Lakes Rally 26–28 August
C. Sainz/L. Moya   555   3rd

Rally Australia 16–19 September
C. McRae/D. Ringer   555   1st
P. Bourne/T. Sircombe   555   4th

Sanremo Rally 9–12 October
C. Sainz/L. Moya   555   2nd
C. McRae/D. Ringer   555   5th

Hong Kong–Peking Rally 22–28 October
P. Bourne/T. Sircombe   555   1st
R. Burns/R. Reid   555   2nd

RAC Rally 20–23 November
C. McRae/D. Ringer   555   1st
C. Sainz/L. Moya   555   Crashed
R. Burns/R. Reid   555   Crashed

Rally of Thailand 3–5 December
R. Burns/R. Reid   555   2nd

1995

Monte Carlo Rally 21–26 January
C. Sainz/L. Moya   555   1st
P. Liatti/A. Alessandrini   555   8th
C. McRae/D. Ringer   555   Crashed

Swedish Rally 10–12 February
C. Sainz/L. Moya   555   Rtd, engine
C. McRae/D. Ringer   555   Rtd, engine
M. Jonsson/J. Johansson 555   Rtd, engine

Rally of Portugal 8–10 March
C. Sainz/L. Moya   555   1st
C. McRae/D. Ringer   555   3rd
R. Burns/R. Reid   555   7th

Tour of Corsica 3–5 May
C. Sainz/L. Moya   555   4th
C. McRae/D. Ringer   555   5th
P. Liatti/A. Alessandrini   555   6th

Rally of Indonesia 7–9 July
C. McRae/D. Ringer   555   1st
P. Bourne/T. Sircombe   555   7th

Rally of New Zealand 27–30 July
C. McRae/D. Ringer   555   1st
P. Bourne/T. Sircombe   555   7th
R. Burns/R. Reid   555   Rtd, electrics

Rally of Malaysia 12–14 August
C. McRae/D. Ringer   555   Crashed
P. Bourne/T. Sircombe   555   Crashed

Rally Australia 15–18 September
C. McRae/D. Ringer   555   2nd
C. Sainz/L. Moya   555   Rtd, overheating
P. Bourne/T. Sircombe   555   Crashed

Hong Kong–Peking Rally 14–20 October
R. Burns/R. Reid   555   3rd
P. Bourne/T. Sircombe   555   4th

Catalonia Rally 23–25 October
C. Sainz/L. Moya   555   1st
C. McRae/D. Ringer   555   2nd
P. Liatti/A. Alessandrini   555   3rd

RAC Rally 19–22 November
C. McRae/D. Ringer   555   1st
C. Sainz/L. Moya   555   2nd
R. Burns/R. Reid   555   3rd

Rally of Thailand 2–4 December
R. Burns/R. Reid   555   3rd
P. Liatti/A.Alessandrini   555   4th
P. Bourne/T. Sircombe   555   5th

1996

Swedish Rally 9–11 February
C. McRae/D. Ringer   555   3rd
K. Eriksson/S. Parmander 555   5th
D. Auriol/B. Occelli   555   10th
P. Liatti/M. Farfoglia   555   12th

Rally of Thailand 3–5 March
C. McRae/D. Ringer   555   1st
K. Eriksson/S. Parmander 555   2nd
P. Liatti/M. Farfoglia   555   3rd

Safari Rally 5–7 April
K. Eriksson/S. Parmander 555   2nd
C. McRae/D. Ringer   555   4th
P. Liatti/M. Farfoglia   555   5th

Rally of Indonesia 10–12 May
P. Liatti/F. Pons   555   2nd
K. Eriksson/S. Parmander 555   Crashed
C. McRae/D. Ringer   555   Crashed

Acropolis Rally 2–4 June
C. McRae/D. Ringer   555   1st
P. Liatti/F. Pons   555   4th
K. Eriksson/S. Parmander 555   5th

Rally of Malaysia 15–17 June
K. Eriksson/S. Parmander 555   1st
P. Liatti/F. Pons   555   Crashed

Rally of Argentina 4–6 July
K. Eriksson/S. Parmander 555   3rd
C. McRae/D. Ringer   555   Crashed

Rally of New Zealand 27–30 July
K. Eriksson/S. Parmander 555   2nd
P. Liatti/F. Pons   555   3rd

1000 Lakes Rally 23–26 August
K. Eriksson/S. Parmander 555   5th
C. McRae/D. Ringer   555   Crashed

Rally Australia 13–16 September
K. Eriksson/S. Parmander 555   2nd
C. McRae/D. Ringer   555   4th
P. Liatti/F. Pons   555   7th

Sanremo Rally 13–16 October
C. McRae/D. Ringer   555   1st
K. Eriksson/S. Parmander 555   5th
P. Liatti/F. Pons   555   Rtd, electrics

Hong Kong–Peking Rally 19–25 October
K. Eriksson/S. Parmander 555   Crashed
P. Liatti/F. Pons   555   Crashed

Catalonia Rally 4–6 November
C. McRae/D. Ringer   555   1st
P. Liatti/F. Pons   555   2nd
K. Eriksson/S. Parmander 555   7th

1997

Monte Carlo Rally 19–22 January
P. Liatti/F. Pons   WRC97   1st
C. McRae/N. Grist   WRC97   Crashed

Swedish Rally 7–10 February
K. Eriksson/S. Parmander WRC97   1st
C. McRae/N. Grist   WRC97   4th

Safari Rally 1–3 March
C. McRae/N. Grist   WRC97   1st
K. Eriksson/S. Parmander WRC97   Rtd, suspension

Rally of Portugal 23–26 March
C. McRae/N. Grist   WRC97   Rtd, engine
K. Eriksson/S. Parmander WRC97   Rtd, engine

Catalonia Rally 14–16 April
P. Liatti/F. Pons   WRC97   2nd
C. McRae/N. Grist   WRC97   4th

Tour of Corsica 5–7 May
C. McRae/N. Grist   WRC97   1st
P. Liatti/F. Pons   WRC97   5th

Rally of Argentina 22–24 May
C. McRae/N. Grist   WRC97   2nd
K. Eriksson/S. Parmander WRC97   3rd

Acropolis Rally 8–10 June
C. McRae/N. Grist   WRC97   Rtd, steering
K. Eriksson/S. Parmander WRC97   Rtd, steering

China Rally 21–23 June
C. McRae/N. Grist   WRC97 1st
K. Eriksson/S. Parmander WRC97 2nd

Rally of New Zealand 2–5 August
K. Eriksson/S. Parmander WRC97 1st
C. McRae/N. Grist   WRC97 Rtd, engine

Rally Finland 29–31 August
C. McRae/N. Grist   WRC97 Rtd, engine
K. Eriksson/S. Parmander WRC97 Rtd, engine

Rally of Indonesia 19–21 September
K. Eriksson/S. Parmander WRC97 3rd
C. McRae/N. Grist   WRC97 Rtd, accident damage

Sanremo Rally 12–15 October
C. McRae/N. Grist   WRC97 1st
P. Liatti/F. Pons   WRC97 2nd

Rally Australia 30 October–2 November
C. McRae/N. Grist   WRC97 1st
K. Eriksson/S. Parmander WRC97 Crashed

RAC Rally 23–25 November
C. McRae/N. Grist   WRC97 1st
P. Liatti/F. Pons   WRC97 7th
K. Eriksson/S. Parmander WRC97 Rtd, engine

1998

Monte Carlo Rally 19–21 January
C. McRae/N. Grist   WRC98 3rd
P. Liatti/F. Pons   WRC98 4th

Swedish Rally 6–8 February
K. Eriksson/S. Parmander WRC98 4th
C. McRae/N. Grist   WRC98 Rtd, electrics

Safari Rally 28 February–2 March
C. McRae/N. Grist   WRC98 Rtd, engine
P. Liatti/F. Pons   WRC98 Rtd, engine

Rally of Portugal 22–25 March
C. McRae/N. Grist   WRC98 1st
P. Liatti/F. Pons   WRC98 6th

Catalonia Rally 20–22 April
C. McRae/N. Grist   WRC98 Rtd, transmission
P. Liatti/F. Pons   WRC98 Crashed

Tour of Corsica 4–6 May
C. McRae/N. Grist   WRC98 1st
P. Liatti/F. Pons   WRC98 3rd

Rally of Argentina 20–23 May
C. McRae/N. Grist   WRC98 5th
P. Liatti/F. Pons   WRC98 6th

Acropolis Rally 7–9 June
C. McRae/N. Grist   WRC98 1st
P. Liatti/F. Pons   WRC98 6th

China Rally 20–22 June
C. McRae/N. Grist   WRC98 1st
P. Liatti/F. Pons   WRC98 2nd

Rally of New Zealand 24–27 July
C. McRae/N. Grist   WRC98 5th
P. Liatti/F. Pons   WRC98 6th

Rally Finland 21–23 August
J. Kytolehto/A. Kapanen   WRC98 8th
C. McRae/N. Grist   WRC98 Rtd, accident damage

Sanremo Rally 12–14 October
P. Liatti/F. Pons   WRC98 2nd
C. McRae/N. Grist   WRC98 3rd

Rally Australia 4–7 November
C. McRae/N. Grist   WRC98 4th
P. Liatti/F. Pons   WRC98 Crashed

Rally of Great Britain 22–24 November
C. McRae/N. Grist	WRC98	Rtd, engine
A. McRae/D. Senior	WRC98	Crashed
A. Vatanen/F. Pons	WRC98	Rtd, engine

1999

Monte Carlo Rally 17–20 January
J. Kankkunen/J. Repo	WRC98	2nd
B. Thiry/S. Prevot	WRC98	5th
R. Burns/R. Reid	WRC98	8th

Swedish Rally 12–14 February
R. Burns/R. Reid	WRC99	5th
J. Kankkunen/J. Repo	WRC99	6th
B. Thiry/S. Prevot	WRC99	10th

Safari Rally 25–28 February
J. Kankkunen/J. Repo	WRC99	Rtd, electrics
B. Thiry/S. Prevot	WRC99	Rtd, electrics
R. Burns/R. Reid	WRC99	Rtd, suspension

Rally of Portugal 21–24 March
R. Burns/R. Reid	WRC99	4th
B. Thiry/S. Prevot	WRC99	6th
J. Kankkunen/J. Repo	WRC99	Rtd, engine

Catalonia Rally 19–24 April
R. Burns/R. Reid	WRC98	5th
J. Kankkunen/J. Repo	WRC99	6th
B. Thiry/S. Prevot	WRC99	7th

Tour of Corsica 7–9 May
R. Burns/R. Reid	WRC99	7th
B. Thiry/S. Prevot	WRC99	Crashed

Rally of Argentina 22–25 May
J. Kankkunen/J. Repo	WRC99	1st
R. Burns/R. Reid	WRC99	2nd

Acropolis Rally 6–9 June
R. Burns/R. Reid	WRC99	1st
J. Kankkunen/J. Repo	WRC99	Rtd, suspension

Rally of New Zealand 15–18 July
J. Kankkunen/J. Repo	WRC99	2nd
R. Burns/R. Reid	WRC99	Rtd, gearbox

Rally Finland 20–22 August
J. Kankkunen/J. Repo	WRC99	1st
R. Burns/R. Reid	WRC99	2nd

China Rally 16–19 September
R. Burns/R. Reid	WRC99	2nd
J. Kankkunen/J. Repo	WRC99	4th

Sanremo Rally 11–13 October
R. Burns/R. Reid	WRC99	Crashed
J. Kankkunen/J. Repo	WRC99	6th

Rally Australia 4–7 November
R. Burns/R. Reid	WRC99	1st
J. Kankkunen/J. Repo	WRC99	Rtd, suspension

Rally of Great Britain 21–23 November
R. Burns/R. Reid	WRC99	1st
J. Kankkunen/J. Repo	WRC99	2nd

2000

Monte Carlo Rally 20–22 January
J. Kankkunen/J. Repo	WRC99	2nd
R. Burns/R. Reid	WRC99	Rtd, electrics

Swedish Rally 10–13 February
R. Burns/R. Reid	WRC99	5th
J. Kankkunen/J. Repo	WRC99	6th

Safari Rally 25–27 February
R. Burns/R. Reid	WRC99	1st
J. Kankkunen/J. Repo	WRC99	2nd

Rally of Portugal 17–19 March
R. Burns/R. Reid	WRC00	1st
J. Kankkunen/J. Repo	WRC00	Crashed

Catalonia Rally 31 March–2 April
R. Burns/R. Reid	WRC00	2nd
J. Kankkunen/J. Repo	WRC00	Rtd

Rally of Argentina 11–14 May
R. Burns/R. Reid	WRC00	1st
J. Kankkunen/J. Repo	WRC00	4th

Acropolis Rally 9–11 June
J. Kankkunen/J. Repo	WRC00	3rd
R. Burns/R. Reid	WRC00	Rtd, engine

Rally of New Zealand 13–16 July
R. Burns/R. Reid	WRC00	Rtd, engine
J. Kankkunen/J. Repo	WRC00	Rtd, engine

Rally Finland 18–20 August
R. Burns/R. Reid	WRC00	Crashed
J. Kankkunen/J. Repo	WRC00	8th

Cyprus Rally 8–10 September
R. Burns/R. Reid	WRC00	4th
J. Kankkunen/J. Repo	WRC00	7th

Tour of Corsica 29 September–1 October
R. Burns/R. Reid	WRC00	4th
S. Jean-Joseph/J. Boyère	WRC00	7th

Sanremo Rally 20–22 October
S. Jean-Joseph/J. Boyère	WRC00	7th
R. Burns/R. Reid	WRC00	Rtd, accident damage

Rally Australia 9–12 November
R. Burns/R. Reid	WRC00	2nd
J. Kankkunen/J. Repo	WRC00	Crashed
P. Solberg/P. Mills	WRC00	Crashed
M. Märtin/M. Park	WRC00	Rtd, transmission

Rally of Great Britain 24–26 November
R. Burns/R. Reid	WRC99	1st
J. Kankkunen/J. Repo	WRC00	5th
P. Solberg/P. Mills	WRC00	Crashed

2001

Monte Carlo Rally 18–20 January
R. Burns/R. Reid	WRC01	Rtd, engine
P. Solberg/P. Mills	WRC01	Crashed
M. Märtin/M. Park	WRC01	Rtd, engine

Swedish Rally 10–13 February
P. Solberg/P. Mills	WRC01	6th
M. Märtin/M. Park	WRC01	12th
R. Burns/R. Reid	WRC01	16th

Rally of Portugal 8–11 March
R. Burns/R. Reid	WRC01	4th
P. Solberg/P. Mills	WRC01	Rtd, suspension
M. Märtin/M. Park	WRC01	Crashed

Catalonia Rally 23–25 March
R. Burns/R. Reid	WRC01	7th
P. Solberg/P. Mills	WRC01	Crashed
M. Märtin/M. Park	WRC01	Rtd, gearbox

Rally of Argentina 3–6 May
R. Burns/R. Reid	WRC01	2nd
P. Solberg/P. Mills	WRC01	5th

Cyprus Rally 1–3 June
R. Burns/R. Reid	WRC01	2nd
T. Arai/G. Macneall	WRC01	4th
P. Solberg/P. Mills	WRC01	Rtd, fire

Acropolis Rally 15–17 June
P. Solberg/P. Mills	WRC01	2nd
R. Burns/R. Reid	WRC01	Rtd, propshaft
M. Märtin/M. Park	WRC01	Rtd, suspension

Safari Rally 20–22 July
R. Burns/R. Reid	WRC01	Rtd, suspension
P. Solberg/P. Mills	WRC01	Rtd, wheel bearing
T. Arai/G. Macneall	WRC01	Rtd, suspension

Rally Finland 24–26 August
R. Burns/R. Reid	WRC01	2nd
M. Märtin/M. Park	WRC01	5th
P. Solberg/P. Mills	WRC01	7th

Rally of New Zealand 20–23 September
R. Burns/R. Reid	WRC01	1st,
P. Solberg/P. Mills	WRC01	7th
T. Arai/G. Macneall	WRC01	14th

Sanremo Rally 4–7 October
P. Solberg/P. Mills	WRC01	9th
R. Burns/R. Reid	WRC01	Crashed
M. Märtin/M. Park	WRC01	Crashed

Tour of Corsica 19–21 October
R. Burns/R. Reid	WRC01	4th
P. Solberg/P. Mills	WRC01	5th
M. Märtin/M. Park	WRC01	6th

Rally Australia 1–4 November
R. Burns/R. Reid	WRC01	2nd
P. Solberg/P. Mills	WRC01	7th
T. Arai/G. Macneall	WRC01	Crashed

Rally of Great Britain 23–25 November
R. Burns/R. Reid	WRC01	3rd
T. Arai/G. Macneall	WRC01	10th
P. Solberg/P. Mills	WRC01	Rtd, fuel system
M. Märtin/M. Park	WRC01	Rtd, engine

2002

Monte Carlo Rally 18–20 January
T. Makinen/K. Lindstrom	WRC01	1st
P. Solberg/P. Mills	WRC01	6th

Swedish Rally 31 January–3 February
T. Makinen/K. Lindstrom	WRC01	Rtd, engine
P. Solberg/P. Mills	WRC01	Rtd, engine

Tour of Corsica 8–10 March
P. Solberg/P. Mills	WRC02	5th
T. Makinen/K. Lindstrom	WRC02	Crashed

Catalonia Rally 21–24 March
P. Solberg/P. Mills	WRC02	5th
T. Makinen/K. Lindstrom	WRC02	Rtd, engine

Cyprus Rally 19–21 April
T. Makinen/K. Lindstrom	WRC02	3rd
P. Solberg/P. Mills	WRC02	5th

Rally of Argentina 16–19 May
P. Solberg/P. Mills	WRC02	2nd
T. Makinen/K. Lindstrom	WRC02	Crashed

Acropolis Rally 13–16 June
P. Solberg/P. Mills	WRC02	5th
T. Makinen/K. Lindstrom	WRC02	Crashed

Safari Rally 11–14 July
P. Solberg/P. Mills	WRC02	Rtd, engine
T. Makinen/K. Lindstrom	WRC02	Rtd, suspension

Rally Finland 8–11 August
P. Solberg/P. Mills	WRC02	3rd
T. Makinen/K. Lindstrom	WRC02	5th

Deutschland Rally 22–25 August
T. Makinen/K. Lindstrom	WRC02	7th
P. Solberg/P. Mills	WRC02	Crashed
T. Arai/A. Sircombe	WRC02	Rtd, gearbox
A. Mörtl/K. Wicha	WRC02	Crashed

Sanremo Rally 19–22 September
P. Solberg/P. Mills	WRC02	3rd
T. Makinen/K. Lindstrom	WRC02	Rtd, driveshaft
A. Mörtl/K. Wicha	WRC02	Withdrawn

Rally of New Zealand 3–6 October
T. Makinen/K. Lindstrom	WRC02	3rd
P. Solberg/P. Mills	WRC02	Rtd, engine

Rally Australia 31 October–3 November
P. Solberg/P. Mills	WRC02	3rd
T. Makinen/K. Lindstrom	WRC02	Excluded

Rally of Great Britain 14–17 November
P. Solberg/P. Mills	WRC02	1st
T. Makinen/K. Lindstrom	WRC02	4th

2003

Monte Carlo Rally 23–26 January
P. Solberg/P. Mills	WRC03	Crashed
T. Makinen/K. Lindstrom	WRC03	Crashed

Swedish Rally 7–9 February
T. Makinen/K. Lindstrom	WRC03	2nd
P. Solberg/P. Mills	WRC03	6th

Rally of Turkey 27 February–2 March
T. Makinen/K. Lindstrom	WRC03	8th
P. Solberg/P. Mills	WRC03	Rtd, broken steering

Rally of New Zealand 10–13 April
P. Solberg/P. Mills   WRC03 3rd
T. Makinen/K. Lindstrom   WRC03 7th

Rally of Argentina 8–11 May
P. Solberg/P. Mills   WRC03 5th
T. Makinen/K. Lindstrom   WRC03 Withdrawn

Acropolis Rally 5–8 June
P. Solberg/P. Mills   WRC03 3rd
T. Makinen/K. Lindstrom   WRC03 5th

Cyprus Rally 20–22 June
P. Solberg/P. Mills   WRC03 1st
T. Makinen/K. Lindstrom   WRC03 Rtd, OTL

Deutschland Rally 24–27 July
P. Solberg/P. Mills   WRC03 8th
T. Makinen/K. Lindstrom   WRC03 Rtd, electrics

Rally Finland 7–10 August
P. Solberg/P. Mills   WRC03 2nd
T. Makinen/K. Lindstrom   WRC03 6th

Rally Australia 4–7 September
P. Solberg/P. Mills   WRC03 1st
T. Makinen/K. Lindstrom   WRC03 6th

Sanremo Rally 3–5 October
T. Makinen/K. Lindstrom   WRC03 10th
P. Solberg/P. Mills   WRC03 Rtd, no fuel

Tour of Corsica 17–19 October
P. Solberg/P. Mills   WRC03 1st
T. Makinen/K. Lindstrom   WRC03 7th

Catalonia Rally 23–26 October
P. Solberg/P. Mills   WRC03 5th
T. Makinen/K. Lindstrom   WRC03 8th

Rally of Great Britain 6–9 November
P. Solberg/P. Mills   WRC03 1st
T. Makinen/K. Lindstrom   WRC03 3rd

2004

Monte Carlo Rally 23–25 January
P. Solberg/P. Mills   WRC03 7th
M. Hirvonen/J. Lehtinen   WRC03 Crashed

Swedish Rally 6–8 February
P. Solberg/P. Mills   WRC03 3rd
M. Hirvonen/J. Lehtinen   WRC03 9th

Rally Mexico 12–14 March
P. Solberg/P. Mills   WRC04 4th
M. Hirvonen/J. Lehtinen   WRC04 5th

Rally of New Zealand 15–18 April
P. Solberg/P. Mills   WRC04 1st
M. Hirvonen/J. Lehtinen   WRC04 7th

Cyprus Rally 14–16 May
P. Solberg/P. Mills   WRC04 6th
M. Hirvonen/J. Lehtinen   WRC04 7th

Acropolis Rally 4–6 June
P. Solberg/P. Mills   WRC04 1st
M. Hirvonen/J. Lehtinen   WRC04 Crashed

Rally of Turkey 24–27 June
P. Solberg/P. Mills   WRC04 3rd
M. Hirvonen/J. Lehtinen   WRC04 6th

Rally of Argentina 15–18 July
P. Solberg/P. Mills   WRC04 Rtd, engine
M. Hirvonen/J. Lehtinen   WRC04 4th

Rally Finland 6–8 August
P. Solberg/P. Mills   WRC04 Crashed
M. Hirvonen/J. Lehtinen   WRC04 Crashed

Deutschland Rally 20–22 August
P. Solberg/P. Mills   WRC04 Crashed
M. Hirvonen/J. Lehtinen   WRC04 8th

Rally Japan 3–5 September
P. Solberg/P. Mills   WRC04 1st
M. Hirvonen/J. Lehtinen   WRC04 7th

Index